The Psychology of Hip Hop

The Psychology of Hip Hop

Terence McPhaul, M.A., N.C.S.C.

iUniverse, Inc.
New York Lincoln Shanghai

The Psychology of Hip Hop

iUniverse books may be ordered through booksellers or by contacting:

iUniverse
2021 Pine Lake Road, Suite 100
Lincoln, NE 68512
www.iuniverse.com
1-800-Authors (1-800-288-4677)

ISBN-13: 978-0-595-35152-7 (pbk)
ISBN-13: 978-0-595-79853-7 (ebk)
ISBN-10: 0-595-35152-2 (pbk)
ISBN-10: 0-595-79853-5 (ebk)

Printed in the United States of America

Contents

ACKNOWLEDGEMENTS

This was an arduous process, and it would not have been possible without the help and encouragement of some very special people. First, I would like to thank my mother Cheryl K. McPhaul, the most fearless and courageous person I know, and who taught me everything that allowed me to make it this far. To her I owe my education, the business, this book and my life. Thank you for being the type of person who does not run from tough situations, but who can take life by the horns and tame it. Thanks for achieving the impossible and blazing new paths for those who lacked the vision.

John, Mary, Grover, Ralph, Tremayne and Jacinta you all make me so very proud because each of you conquers the world piece by piece every day. I like that when something difficult arises, instead of whining about what has to be done you chip away at an obstacle until it completely disappears. In addition, the family has grown stronger and brighter because of the care, compassion, intelligence, wisdom and common sense that you have all used in raising your children. We are all better off with Jermaine, DuJuan, Demetrius, Arthur III (Trey), Shauntay, Roderick, Cheryl (Nikki), Eric, Olivia, Alyssa, Tremayne, Jr. (Bailey), Mahogany, Tremarius, Ricardo, Paige and Ahman. Keep on doing what you do. I love you! Eileen, Sheri, Anita and Nyrae, Anita, Chaka, Patti, Maya, Celine, Damon, Faith, Trina, Lila, Steven, Morgan, Blake, Tina, Little Richard, Cher, Shania, Luther and Madonna, thanks to you too!

There are some very special friends I must recognize, and certainly they have no idea how much they mean to me, and how they have positively shaped my life over the years. Brian Bowers, Sean Boyd, Kevin William Carter, Michelle Fai, William B. Davis III, Ralinda Jones, Reginald Newport, and Jeffrey B. Alston, many blessings for your direction, love and patience.

And to the Griffith family (Belinda, Bernard, Corey, and Phillip), my life is so much more fulfilled by your friendship, support and love. The inspiration that you provide is with me daily, and honestly, I can say that the music you make as a family is of the purest kind, and each of my days begins and ends with the sound of it. Remember, there is much more to come!

My mentor, Dr. Eugene Herrington, who has provided me with so much inspiration and led me to so much knowledge. Still the best psychologist I know, and as I have mentioned before, often fueled conversations that were precursors for my writings. The perfect blend of the theoretical, practical and applicable processes of psychology, I am much better off professionally and personally having met you, and having studied under your tutelage.

IN LOVING MEMORY

Mary Frances Baker (1924-1982) who provided me with my first introduction to the field of psychology, and who taught me that in any situation there is a "silver lining." I remember homemade doughnuts and hot apple cider at Halloween, hot chocolate after neighborhood Christmas caroling, routine picnics at the Detroit River, and discipline every day.

And Arthur Wilbur McPhaul, Jr. (1961-2000), who was taken from this world much too early by a senseless act of violence. My big brother, who believed me to be a bright star when no one else did.

CULTURAL FACTORS

One may still find it fascinating that hip hop music and culture has reached so many people in terms of its popularity. Fortune 500 companies use its music and the recording artists in their advertising. And the hip hop colloquialisms have discretely infiltrated the scripts of primetime television shows and programs specifically designed for any other culture than African Americans. One might say that hip hop has ascended barriers that previously isolated the genre, and "its kind."

The fact of the matter is that there exists a precarious dichotomy related to the thought patterns of African Americans, and everyone else related to hip hop and its attached culture. The fundamental difference appears to be that African Americans see hip hop as an unchanging lifestyle, while everyone else sees hip hop as entertainment.

Absolutely remarkable, is that those from other cultures only wish to be entertained by hip hop. Many feel that the music is great for nightclubs and for sassy and dysfunctional characters on television, but the stance is hardly useful for anything more. Is this not the reason that whites have been interested in all culture derived from the African continent, because it has an "exotic nature?"

It appears that the same still happens today. Let's take for example that one has a Caucasian male, college graduate, who obtains a position as an international banker with a global bank. This individual enjoys hanging out in the nightclubs, as many new executives do, after a hard day's work. He loves the music being played, which is "active radio format". Which translates to tunes to which many feel they can dance to; and much of the *perceived* "hottest" tunes fall within the hip hop framework (i.e. including Britney, Christina, Snoop, 50Cent). The difference between he and his African American cohort is that the Caucasian male understands that it is entertainment, and that the lingo and culture in its entirety is not transferable to mainstream society.

Many view this as a negative mainstream society. And those of the hip hop cadre indicate that those who do not truly live the lifestyle are not "keeping it real." The problem is that in much of the African American culture, hip hop has created such negative connotations, that are accepted and understood as such; while Caucasians may indicate that glorification of cop killing, raping, burgling, burning bodies, selling illicit drugs, and exploitation of women is not appropriate. There are some African Americans who actually believe that there is something wrong with not being able to speak standard hip hop on the job. Furthermore, those African Americans who do use the English language are said to be "trying to be white," "not keeping it real," or they are "uncle Toms." It is believed that the white man is simply trying to "keep the black man down," if he is not able to just be himself. Some would have everyone believe that baggy jeans and overpriced Timberland boots, and Air Jordan's should be part of the corporate uniform.

One argument purported is that people who make this music (mind you not everyone) has lived the hip hop lifestyle, and that the music is simply a chronicle of the everyday happenings within and throughout the ghetto. So in other words these individuals are just "keeping it real." The fact of the matter is that since record companies are targeting rebellious adolescents, and in many cases irresponsibly, this is the reason the music tends to be made. It is a multibillion dollar a year industry. And in this process the African American culture is being scarificed because the only message that is getting to the public, through the music, is that African Americans are murderers, drug dealers and thieves. Moreover, in these images African American women are worthless.

Record companies are willing to perpetuate this because it sells records, but even the more rebellious Caucasians realize the difference between entertainment and lifestyle. Do those making money really care? No. Because, they really do not understand **THE** implications or ramifications. After theses millionaire entertainers make it big they certainly are not going back to the neighborhood to live.

In all fairness there are a few of the hip hop performers who started foundations and they provide limited assistance to their old communities. Ludacris does a lot of work in communities around the country with his Ludacris Kids Foundation. Nelly does the same. However, other than a few Christmas gifts, or a turkey once a year, those most impacted by the negative images perpetuated by hip hop will never be assisted to a great deal.

How often would one suppose that hip hop artists go back to the communities from whence they came, and develop programs that have a long lasting effect? Programs that are designed to diminish the less than sanguine circumstances? Do these hip hoppers truly want to improve the circumstances of the community (ghetto) as they purport? If someone really wanted to help, would not there be more in the trenches doing serious work that will impact the community, and keep young men and women from living out the deceptions that are so pervasive in the videos? How much is education really pushed, teen pregnancy pointed out as a devastating plague within the African American community? Well, Let's just say that one is more likely to see a video of bare chests and bare backsides, sliding up and down poles. Underage and impressionable young men are encouraged to engage because if they in fact exploit women, it is somehow a declaration of their manhood. Ridiculous isn't it? However, women are encouraged to submit. The record companies that earn billions off of these images fail even more miserably to provide relief to the communities that suffer most from the images.

Another puzzling element is the influence that hip hop has on the African American who has not had to live the images glorified in the music and associated videos. I put forth this idea to a group of college students at a large Historically Black College. Many indicated that they subscribe to the images and messages in hip hop because they are "keeping it real." This can certainly be expected of those individuals who developed from meager circumstances, but one of the most vocal students was the product of two parents who were medical doctors. My response to this was that if one is "keeping it real" would it not make more sense for such a person to "keep it real" by being a responsible citizen, performing above average in school, and perhaps follow in his parents footsteps? What about taking more time to learn more about African American culture and finding ways to disseminate positive images?

Looking further, often parents contribute to the mayhem, and there are more sinister implications to contend with. To me it is always disturbing to hear parents refer to their children's clothing as "sexy".

Young women bombarded with these images and highly impressionable do begin to subscribe to the visuals because they are presented as glamorous. When adults justify certain images, matters are just made worse.

Video programs and radio stations are less responsible than warranted because the stations which target African Americans, in contrast to Caucasians allow more offensive and inappropriate material to be televised during the time that impressionable children are likely to hear and see it. It is my belief, as well as the notion of others, that radio and television programmers are going to be responsible enough to divert certain programming out of the reach of children during those times when they are likely to have access to a television. For whites this is usually true. For programs targeting African Americans, and those stations where certain content can be found, it is apparent that a total disregard for African American children is prevalent. Somewhere along there line there exists a false belief that was somehow nurtured, that it is alright to expose African American children to negative images. But is this not what was done during the days of slavery, and since? Were not small children abused when they were forced to work in the fields of the south, beaten and often raped. The same, however, was never deemed suitable for a white child.

African Americans must make programmers responsible-and hold them accountable by the community voicing its concerns over the travesties woven within the white run entertainment industry. The parents of white children are quick to do it. The entertainment industry argues that it listens to all complaints, but those coming from African Americans often fall on deaf ears, even to programmers at Black Entertainment Television. But, Black Entertainment Television is a white owned company too. How can one reasonably think that it is airtight to see teenage boys seduced by grown women, or the boys to see that once they make money, they will be able to have women slide up and downs poles all day; that sexual decadence is the ultimate status symbol?

While there are natural occurrences in the development of males and females, there are certain elements they understand, and certain delineations in the developmental process that children have to be schooled about. Parents must be available to explain things about which children are likely to have questions. However, there are some images children should never see. This is sometimes a difficult task, and this is why the status of being a parent is called "parenting" instead of "visiting" children.

EAST COAST V. WEST COAST

The media has helped in concocting this overwhelmingly intense idea, that there is a huge war going on within the hip hop community, which pits east coast performers against west coast performers. As we all know, the media does tend to be histrionic in its approach to delivering the news; and sometimes creating what does not exist. Perhaps there are a few performers who engage in feuds, and they just happen to be hip hop performers. To go even further, one of the performers may be from the east coast, and one may hail from the west coast. However, these specifications alone do not add up to a turf war that is the equivalent to Cesar's conquests.

It is no secret that the African American community, mostly, has criticized the media for creating destructive images of African Americans and the hip hop community. This was further substantiated with television news, radio, advertising and television programming; whites control all of the mediums. Seldom can an African American gain a life sustaining role on television in daytime or primetime, unless they are stooges. For various reasons, it was in the best interest of a few to perpetuate the images of uneducated, disrespectful and violent thugs who lacked direction and could not gain any, unless there was intervention from a "good white person." In many cases, the only idea that permeates the psyche of most of the world is that African Americans are a lost cause. Heretofore the focus has been on images contrived by the media. There is no doubt hip hop has become consistently more popular across populations and cultures. The hip hop community has certain key figures such as Death Row president, Marion "Suge" Knight and record producer, media mogul, fashion designer, and partygoer extraordinaire Sean "P. Diddy" Combs. Both are successful businessmen, even though strong-arming by both has been alleged. One would be hard pressed to be able to list their accomplishments without being able to name a high profile scandal, which has been tainted and embellished with some violence.

Everyone remembers the Club New York incident with Combs that ensnarled the ultra feminine and stellar business tycoon, Jennifer Lopez. Lopez was smart in that she unglued herself from the scandal. What's more, this one incident caused Combs to hire Johnny Cochran. In addition the rap career of Jamaal "Shyne" Barrow was stalled due to the mayhem that occurred that night. Subsequently, Combs abandoned his protégé.

Lest the world forget the bat wielding Combs, when Steve Stoute was nearly killed at the hands of Combs and his band of merry thugs; the kind who rob the poor and keep getting rich.

The havoc in 1992 involving Combs is still being settled today via civil litigation. For those unfamiliar, in 1992, three people died at an event hosted by Combs. This event somehow exceeded capacity, and ultimately an altercation erupted. Anarchy exploded and many attendees were trampled, some to their death. Legal haggling has continued since. Why? Why were the families of the dead and injured not simply compensated for their losses? Why did Combs not serve any jail time for his part in this devastating spectacle? Did he have "the hook-up?" Equally disturbing is the history of Knight. Everyone is likely familiar with the "Vanilla Ice" incident. The allegation was that "Suge" held "Vanilla Ice" outside a window by his ankles, high above the city street until he conceded to "Suge's" demands regarding a recording contract. Shortly thereafter, the platinum selling rapper "Vanilla Ice" lost his fervor for rap music.

Knight has served time in prison, and is considered a hardened felon. Knight has bragged about being a "strong arm" and a drug dealer with undeniable connections to an L.A. gang, the "Bloods". Knight has a history of using intimidation to subdue his adversaries, and the general public. There are some members of the press who fear his presence. Knight exudes the aura that danger is imminent. One female interviewer disclosed that she was fearful at one point, that she would be raped by Knight and his chain of half-wits.

Knight even made his way to the Vibe Awards, and this resulted in the awards being postponed, just long enough to get the crowds under control. It was alleged that Knight initiated an attack against one of the awardees in attendance at the event. Several altercations blossomed, knives were drawn, and someone was stabbed. Of course, it was a rapper who was charged with the stabbing. "Young Buck", who is an up and coming rapper of reasonable talent, issued the bloody strike. Afterwards he stayed on the lamb eventually turning himself in to authorities. Mind you, only the highest profile cases make the news. What about those people upon whom intimidation is successful? The public will likely never hear such stories.

What hip hop has made evident, is that the genre and those who subscribe to its lifestyle tenets display nothing more than Antisocial Personality Disorder. This condition is not what many perceive it to be. Antisocial Personality Disorder, is not the condition whereby individuals do not want to be around others. According to the Diagnostic and Statistical Manual of Mental Disorders Antisocial Personality Disorder is a condition in which an individual has a complete disregard for, and violates the rights of others. This condition usually begins in a milder form (Oppositional Defiant Disorder) in childhood. When the condition is not treated it becomes increasingly worse as one progresses toward adulthood.

Individuals with Antisocial Personality Disorder are savvy about rationalizing that upon people whom they brought harm somehow deserved it. Personas with Antisocial Personality Disorder are emotionally cold and disconnected. It would appear to the onlooker that the person with this disorder has no conscience. This is essentially true because they lack sympathy and empathy no matter what degree of suffering they witness. In essence the condition is sociopath.

One may question just how such a condition arises. Largely parenting is to blame for such outcomes. Inconsistent parenting and insufficient role models provide the perfect condition for breeding the Antisocial Personality. Inconsistent parenting can occur when parents rear children from completely separate points of reference so that the child receives mixed messages. For instance, if a child acts out negatively and there is an n established form of punishment in place, such as not allowing a child to watch television in the evening and one parent does not honor this arrangement the child learns to triangulate. Meaning the child learns that rules to not apply. One can simply go to the source that does not enforce the rules. The conditions associated with the Antisocial condition, such as Oppositional Defiant Disorder can be seem fully developed by the age of five. If something is not exacted to treat the condition, the disruptive fallout continues and the behavior worsens by the time the child reaches adolescence. At adolescence the name changes to Conduct Disorder.

In all of these conditions it is not unusual that other disorders co-exist. Depression, substance abuse and chemical dependence are common. Being that many of the hip hop artists start their craft very early it is not surprising that one sees drug use manifested. Especially given the fact that such behavior is encouraged and worn by the elders as a badge of honor. There tends to be excessive consumption of marijuana amongst this group, which only exacerbates certain underlying conditions. Marijuana is a hallucinogen and studies show an increased rate of delinquent behavior, violence, depression and suicide amongst youngsters who partake in the activity.

The entire concept of creating a psychopath is not really hard to understand. Consider that in the African American community, single parent households continue to be on the rise. In many cases grandparents, love interests and others tend to share in the disciplinary procedures related to raising the children. These folks who are most interested in the child's welfare rarely come together to develop a long-term plan for the irrigation and bloom of appropriate behaviors. More often than not, mixed messages to the children are sent because the adults, and/or parental figures are not on one accord.

Parents are getting increasingly younger with ten, eleven and twelve year olds becoming pregnant. Parents, who are not waiting to have children until they are adults, when they are more experienced at life, usually have significant difficulty raising their children. It is virtually impossible that these kids who are now parents, with limited intellectual, emotional and social skills, will be able to raise a child during the baby's most formative period. These baby parents are more likely to be fans of hip hop as well, and have a propensity to be able to expose their babies to images of drugs, violence and sexual promiscuity. Another dilemma is that often pressure to raise children born of children falls on the shoulders of grandparents, who thought they were in a point in their own lives where they could simply bask in the peace and quite associated with not having to wake in the middle of the night to change diapers and feed the brood.

These new grandparents are rarely in the mood to raise children who were completely unexpected. Once the grandparent assumes the responsibility of the grandchildren, tension mounts with their own child. This very prospect is ominous because all involved would like to remain in denial. Children who witness the poor social structure in the household, especially when the grandchild sees his/her own parent treated as a child, the grandchild fails to grow sufficient respect for their own parent. The grandchild has a sibling relationship with their parent, as opposed to guardian figure. This contributes to the confusion regarding the role of the authority figure.

Crack cocaine completely ravaged the African American community. Furthermore, many of the gangster images simply glorified the lifestyle of selling crack cocaine. It is sad when children perceive a drug dealer as a hero because he has a flashy car, jewelry and clothes that draw notable attention. How does a hard working parent of meager circumstances compete? While there are ways, the task is easier said than done. Even though many of these same children were aware that their own parents were victims of crack cocaine, they could not resist the temptation to earn a fast buck; risking moral, social and emotional death.

Considering that a company such as Murder Inc. has a CEO who continued to deal drugs, and laundered money it is clear just how strong such an emotional sickness can be. Irv Gotti's record label earned hundreds of millions of dollars, yet, instead of moving his focus to more legitimate means of enterprise, it appears that he has been more willing to languish in a life of crime. Does this likely mean that participating in crime is a more powerful medium, or provides a more powerful image in the African American community? Probably.

Murder Inc, has continued to operate an international enterprise of drugs, extortion, and some have alleged, murder. It was even rumored, that one of the core businesses of Murder Inc. was "murder for hire." Gotti did not have to continue to engage in such behavior, but to him and his cronies, the idea remained glamorous.

Amazing is the depth to which everyone was willing to buy into the East Coast v. West Coast fairy tale concerning the deaths of Christopher "Notorious B.I.G." Wallace and Tupac Shakur. Consider that each of the major players in this urban tragedy actually was believed by investigators to have motive to be rid of their respective artists. This is just a theory, but what if the real motives did not lie in revenge or machismo, but greed? Consequently, neither Notorious B.I.G. nor Tupac were pleased with their contractual restraints imposed by their record companies at the times of their deaths. Tupac and Notorious B.I.G. experienced financial disappointments because the deals that were signed with Death Row and Bad Boy Records respectively were far more lucrative for the record companies than they would ever be for the iconic rap stars.

A situation such as this, with the rappers making their feelings public could have proven to be a complete disaster for each of the record companies, and personally for both Sean "P. Diddy" Combs and Marion "Suge" Knight. Neither Combs, nor Knight had signed artists as successful as Notorious B.I.G. or Tupac. It is not uncommon for record companies to have insurance on its recording artists in the event of unfortunate "accidents." Also, many times record deals are structured to give the record company control of music after the death of an artist. Loved ones are often so overwhelmed with grief that rarely will litigation ensue. And especially if the record label is savvy enough to wage a public campaign to look concerned about the matter, by starting trust funds for the family, and writing tributes to the fallen artists. This can be a deflection of the real sentiments involved. Recall Afeni Shakur did engage in a legal battle with Death Row over the masters for Tupac's recordings in which she prevailed. I wonder if it ever appeared suspicious to anyone, that in the short period leading up to the deaths of both Notorious B.I.G. and Tupac, that they were both encouraged to almost live in the studio, churning out product that could be placed on commercial recordings long after their untimely demise? Apparently, it was lucky for somebody.

PERSONALITY DISORDERS

Personality Disorders are generally not cured, per se, but some may dissipate by middle age. There are several types of personality disorders, but I am, for the purpose of this exercise, attempting to outline those which I have encountered working with my client population-celebrities.

Antisocial Personality Disorder, Borderline Personality Disorder, Histrionic Personality Disorder, Paranoid Personality Disorder, Dependent Personality Disorder and Narcissistic Personality Disorder are those, which have been seen among celebrities most frequently. They are simply characterized as follows: The paranoid person is always suspicious of others, the antisocial has a total disregard for others, and often will violate the rights and space of another. Borderlines are generally unstable in terms of relationships, which tend to be stormy, whether platonic or intimate. Histrionics are completely emotional and one can be counted on to consume all possible tenets of attention. The narcissist has an overactive need for attention and most often their self-image, at least that which is displayed is inflated and grandiose.

Perhaps some of this sounds familiar. Well, many of these behaviors are tolerated as they are accepted as usual behaviors of a star whether it is the sports, entertainment, corporate, or idle wealthy celebrity. Often the public will rationalize that the celebrity is simply eccentric. And if those close to the celeb were not so afraid of the person in question, or afraid of being figuratively (in most cases) axed, then the world may have more emotionally tenable celebrities who could more effectively engage their designated acumen.

Personality Disorders can be found throughout most of the population, and often the disorder is celebrated. Many simply do not realize what it is that is being celebrated. There are numerous corporate executives who exhibit personality disorders, and they are praised for such. Look at one key feature of Antisocial Personality Disorder, which is deceit. Do parents not often teach children early on to give a firm handshake, because it is a sign of good character? It does not matter in these discussions if one actually has good character, but merely to appear so. What about looking a person in the eye? Have you not heard that one? How many times are youngsters taught to do this when they meet someone-even when they do not wish to. One is taught through these actions, that character of high regard can be concocted.

When the banker, or the lawyer, or the governor is deceitful do we really complain? No, not really. And for the politician, it is accepted that she may be deceitful. In large numbers, one does not complain about the politician's deceit unless that figure is caught in a scandal, and then individuals begin to sound off. The Bill Clinton, Monica Lewinsky episode. A corporate titan like Bill Gates or Jack Welch can climb the ranks, seek to own the universe, and collapse virtually everything in their paths, and often we say as a public, that their behavior is simply "good business." Some of the behavior may be good business decisions, but consider that a majority of their antics inside their company, outside their companies involve deceit. Jack Welch is a perfect example, because while he was axing employees and pillaging companies, he was as well cheating on his wife; sayeth the divorce court. Ken Lay who headed Enron is another example. Lay's behavior was accepted for many years, even when those very close to him knew that his behavior was a problem. Recall that while Enron was on the verge of demise, he continued to encourage others, including employees to retain their loyalty, as well as encouraged them to buy more shares of stock. And Bill Gates, who only later in his career began to find himself in court more frequently defending allegations about infringing on the rights of others; which has included exacting on the same individuals financial difficulty, or at least refusing to allow them to earn that which they were entitled. The cases mentioned are those that gained notoriety. Imagine the damage done from circumstances going undiscovered.

Stars such as Marion "Suge" Knight and Sean "P. Diddy" Combs are but others who continue to exhibit features of personality disorders, and obviously there is no one close to either of them to assist in curbing the dangerous behaviors. "Suge" and "P. Diddy" tend to share features associated with Narcissistic Personality Disorder; however, they both have prominent features indicative of Antisocial Personality Disorder. The antisocial has some of the following features. With the antisocial personality disorder illegal behavior is a common characteristic, as individuals with this disorder typically do not abide by the law, nor is there any respect for it. Deceit, which may result in conning others for personal profit, and aggressiveness that may lead one to brawls. The safety of others, invariably, is not a concern of the person with this disorder. Failure to show remorse is another identifier.

Marion "Suge" Knight, and Sean "P. Diddy" Combs are believed by many to have paved a path of destruction unparalleled in the entertainment industry. There have been beatings, robberies, shootings, rapes and killings; and yet it still continues. They have fans that love them! Perhaps therapy or medication, or both, is the answer to curbing such behaviors. First, one has to be willing to accept that the pattern of behavior is a problem. If not the person with the condition, someone close to the situation could be the saving grace. It could be a girlfriend, brother, mother, or record company president. Maybe even a lawyer. Those who earn money from the insidious behaviors of Knight and Combs will likely never be honest enough or courageous enough to insist that the inappropriate behaviors cease.

MANAGING SUCCESS AND CELEBRITY

One may question why there would exist a need to manage success and celebrity, but be advised that the institution as we know it, may not be as easy as it seems. When one speaks of managing success and celebrity, what is being referred to is the ability for one to feel comfortable within the realm of fame and fortune, and the ability for one to be able to maintain the celebrity while minimizing negative stress and harmful behavior. Not to mention, being able to avoid scandal.

The news is replete with torrid tales featuring superstars that have been accused of perpetrating assault, rape, theft and even murder. There is a lot of truth to some encounters, while often, because a superstar has a reputation the opportunists will surface from beneath the woodwork. The interesting thing about this is, that many celebrities become very angry when the accusations start to fly about certain indiscretions. However, would there be anything about which to talk if the superstar did not provide ammunition?

In western culture, especially, there exists the propensity to place our celebrities in the highest regard, no matter one's character, or with little consideration thereof. Their pedestals are placed so very high, that it would be impossible for a celeb to not fall off at some point in time. Many forget that celebrities are first human beings. What generally happens, however, is that the individuals who achieve celebrity are never really prepared for it. And often the celebrity is unable to navigate the territory responsibly because there is no plan in place. Everything is "seat of the pants" evolution. Often, years are spent daydreaming about success, and everyone feels that they know what they will do when the snowball swells, and almost always, fame changes things in a significant way. Reality sets in.

The hip hop and sports communities have appeared to be the industries most plagued my scandal in recent years, whether it be Sean "P. Diddy" Combs, Jamaal "Shyne" Barrow, Christopher "Notorious B.I.G." Tupac Shakur, Marion "Suge" Knight, Allen Iverson, Jayson Williams, R. Kelly, Irv Gotti, O.J. Simpson, Young Buck, Ray Lewis or Darryl Strawberry. And the list goes on. Overwhelmingly, the scandal tends to loom wherever there is a young African American star; though scandal is not exclusive to African Americans, as Winona Ryder, Phil Spector, Robert Blake, Billy Bob Thornton, Andy Dick, Tommy and Pamela Lee can attest.

I am aware that many will disagree with what I pronounce here, however, it is a known fact, that many African Americans come from backgrounds where success was not expected. Especially with regard to sports, early on in school athletics, there was never anyone available to groom the athletes and to help them prepare for what they would face. While athletes are very instrumental in helping to win games for their school teams, few were actually nurturing the player to see that he received the necessary emotional fortitude to withstand success at a professional level. The goal was to secure a win for the school or university, and protecting or preparing the player was the objective to the extent that it would be of the advantage of the school.

Consequently, what one could find, while searching the histories of these athletes, is that even when they committed heinous crimes while attending their schools, there was someone, usually a coach, who would stand behind the student player, for what was justified as being "for the good of the team." Often this was done to the long-term detriment of the athlete. Instead of a player learning that there exists a consequence for negative or irresponsible actions, they were taught that they are above the law. And often this is what our centers of "higher learning" have promoted.

Hip hop stars on the other hand, and I am merely speaking based on the cases that I know about, often have come from blighted neighborhoods, and they have had to do most anything to survive from drug dealing, to stealing, to prostitution-males and females. What happens is that someone at some point in time sees an unusual talent and begins to market it. Eventually, the marketing turns into exploitation. Some artists realize the extent of their talent, and know how to control what happens to it and how it is used. Many more do not have a clue. The hip hop artists, and others too, think that their record company is in existence to protect and look after them, but of course, this is not the case. The primary focus of the record company is to look after the record company. One is sadly mistaken if one feels that the record company will always "do the right thing," from the artist's perspective.

The sad part is, that whether one is speaking of a sports figure or hip hop star, there is generally no one in their midst who has the skills necessary to steer the celebrity through the murky waters of fame. Most people who were not famous, or the product of famous parents, had promised their family and friends jobs on their personal teams, largely, not expecting consciously to achieve such commercial greatness. Too often individuals chosen to handle key tasks are not nearly prepared academically or socially to administer such savvy. And the best thing a celebrity can do is to pay their family and friends to stay away from their business affairs when they lack sufficient skills to be involved. Every celebrity knows who they are, and in this instance denial is unbecoming.

In my practice, I have had to at least encourage loved ones of celebrities to get the necessary skills to handle tenets of basic business, and public relations. There is nothing wrong with encouraging one to get formal training when they are going to be handling the business affairs of another. Let's face it, getting formal training should allow them to care for their own livelihood; especially if the celebrity is the only source of money. Someone who truly cares for the well being of the celebrity will rarely complain about this effort.

Public sightings are also an element of the celebrity protocol, which should receive some consideration when bad things happen to the celebrity; usually music, film and sports celebrities. The mishaps generally occur in bars and nightclubs, or in the immediate vicinity thereof. After a night of drinking and partying someone has a little too much perhaps, and before long there is a free-for-all. All of the time it is not the celebrity who is to blame. This is another reason celebrities, like the rest of the world, need to be aware of their surroundings, and take better care of where they go, and with whom. Consider Ray Lewis of the Baltimore Ravens. He went out after the Superbowl in Atlanta to have a great time like everyone else during Superbowl.

The story is that Ray and his party were on their way to their car after bar-hopping and as they were approaching their stretch Lincoln Navigator, they were taunted by a couple of young men. One of Ray's friends went back to confront the hecklers. A fight ensued and afterwards two men lay dead from a pointless altercation. Did not anyone realize, that whatever the alleged taunters said, none of it was worth an altercation that would lead to murder or simple expiration? Far too often baggage is carried along with one that can be only negative. Many celebrities state that they would feel guilty if they were to no longer associate with their old acquaintances. It is said to be "selling out." This is an understandable sentiment, but one must keep in mind, that friends are supposed to have your best interest in mind, and if those friends choose to engage in activities, which would endanger the life, reputation or livelihood of the celebrity, it is only necessary to sever the relationship; at least until one is ready to change negative engagements.

Capitalizing off of one's own celebrity might be a more fruitful approach to entertaining. What I mean by this is that many times the celebrity is eager to be a part of the party, and they go into the community to engage companionship. Not in every case, but in some it might be advantageous for the celebrity to host events at his own domain, where one is more apt to be able to control the environment. Sean Combs not included.

One of my clients indicated that he really liked going to night-clubs, and stated that he would not know how to throw a good party at home. Also, my client stated that he liked being able to "feel normal." This particular person had starred in some very big box office hits, and he could rarely go anywhere without being mobbed by fans. He had been in several nightclub altercations-this was not a welcomed element of public affairs. What I did was give the star a few suggestions. One was that he pick a remote location to host a party that was to take place on a regular basis, and the event would have a changing theme. The first was "Mirage" and it was staged in the middle of the desert. There was a tent set-up as a nightclub, and once inside, no one would imagine that they were not inside a hot L.A. nightclub.

The event has been a success and my client has been able to mingle with all sorts of people without becoming consumed by volatile environments. My client does attend some nightclubs, but states that he is more selective about the places he goes, as his own parties have raised his expectations about what a nightclub should be, and who should be there.

Reacting to every comment that someone makes is a problem for many. Let's understand for Western culture, we prefer our celebrities young, and this may mean that they have not gained the sense that the words of another cannot hurt them. The best thing that one can do when they feel that they are being provoked is to deny the urge to react, and what's more, it is better for the celebrity not to even speak. Simply leave the situation. Simple huh? Often, one does not intend to react, but when one speaks the emotions are ignited. The celebrity has to be aware of this at all times. In my experience, it is the male clients who tend to be more physically responsive to taunts, while females tend to internalize. This too should be addressed.

Hiring the right employees is essential, whether it be lawyers, agents, managers, housekeepers and assistants. One must take the time to do the necessary research on those to be hired. One can talk to the Better Business Bureau, Chamber of Commerce, and many Performance Rights Agencies, Secretary of State, Police Departments, former employers, references and friends. If complaints have been filed about a potential team member it is important to know, and the celebrity can at least inquire about the circumstances during an interview. It is important to note for the celebrity, that a consumer credit report alone, is not necessarily an indicator of whether a person is honest and responsible. Individuals who commit white-collar crimes always have excellent credit, this is why they get jobs in banks, law firms, and other areas where they can gain access to another's money and wreak havoc on someone's finances. Also, a recent study of the nation's largest consumer reporting agency, Equifax, revealed that the agency has a 70% error rate.

Celebrities, mostly males, which are in line with the rest of the nation's population, do not maintain their health, as they should. It is very important, especially for one with a rigorous schedule, to be in tune with one's own body, and to see someone medically on a regular basis so that one may know if some dilemma arises. This is important whether the star is Michael Vick, Dennis Rodman or Jay-Z. Maintaining proper physical and mental health can improve one's endurance. There is a lot of stress, and stressors, which coexist with the responsibility of celebrity. It is important that the celebrity have the opportunity, and use such to process emotions. Denying them does not make them go away. However, what usually happens is that the small stressors are not addressed and they are left to fester like a sore until, other circumstances are unveiled that cannot be ignored. Such has been the case with so many, such as Mary J. Blige, Mariah Carey and Tweet. So many scandals and occasions could be circumvented if this one suggestion were adhered to.

NO WHITE LADY I DON'T WANT YOUR PURSE

Race always tends to be an emotional point with most of society. Particularly in America. Yes, African Americans are supposed to be, at least amongst their white counterparts, equal in this great America. Equal in what way one may ask? Well, African Americans are supposed to be living this dream espoused by Martin Luther King, Jr. The one declaring that the races will function in society in complete harmony. Has this happened yet?

Ask any white person and he/she will vigorously assert that racism no longer exists in contemporary society. Most, if you push, will say that they have positively no idea why African Americans make such a "big deal" out of claims of prejudice and discrimination that underlie racism. These same ideas are exacerbated because individuals from foreign lands come to America and embark on successful business ventures or attain higher levels of education, while African Americans often fail to experience this same level of success. This gap in achievement, which may be interpreted as a gap in access by African Americans, is interpreted through the eyes of Caucasians and disseminated throughout the rest of the world by word of mouth, and more insidiously via media. It used to be that only generations privy to the Jim Crow experience were dangerous to the well-being of African Americans, however, with media outlets such as MTV, which through the vast network of its parent company,

Viacom can distribute images across America and throughout France, Asia and the United Kingdom to a new crop of youngsters. Those who tend to believe what they see on television and seek to emulate it. Years of social education and tolerance can be omnipotently destroyed by television. Revisiting the example of business and educational opportunities, rarely does anyone else, outside of African Americans, consider that the very structure of society in America is an antagonist to African Americans.

Getting an education or obtaining a business loan are much more difficult for African Americans because there is a double standard which has always existed for evaluating African Americans and their ability for success. This double standard whether it be from a bank, or an institution of higher learning, or government body, will most likely be led by white men, who as if suffering from a Dissociative Fuge, vehemently deny prohibiting African Americans from partaking of opportunities, while simultaneously erecting guidelines that in many cases appear insurmountable. Take for example, the music industry. Independent music artists create their own music, package it perfectly, and can even manage to get their songs played on the radio, however, they are "dead in the water" if they are not part of the vast distribution channel which is controlled by companies led by white men. And mind you, hip hop music earns billions every year. Even when an African American is promoted to a position of what is supposed to be significance, it appears that the role is designed to keep other minions in order; and little more. The cash cow, which is hip hop music can only be milked when it is finessed. This is accomplished by providing just enough "bling" to have the recording artist indebted to a record label indefinitely. Large advances, apartments, and cars provided to hip hop legends, and hooligans, must be paid back. Often they are cheated because the company will buy items for the artist and charge it back to the artist at a higher value. Far more than the company paid for such trinkets.

The music industry is full of people, hip hoppers, who challenged the authority of the record company. Those who felt that they were talented enough to strike out solo; distributing their product themselves. What they ended up with is absolutely nothing, except perhaps, more debt. Because they were trampled by the mighty foot of the big record company that asserted its ownership. More often than not, the worst treatment is dealt to African Americans who "get out of line" such as Michael Jackson and Mariah Carey, notwithstanding her marriage to former SONY patriarch Tommy Mottola. Will Botwin and Don Einner of SONY Music may be open enough to discuss this phenomenon, but for now, my calls to them have gone unanswered.

Viking style pummeling of a hip hop artist, who fails to accept his/her place, is not unlike what happened at the beginning of the industrial revolution in Belgium. King Leopold had ordered that slaves, who attempted to run away from the work compound, have their hands and feet severed, so that they could no longer escape. Furthermore, these slaves were placed on display by occupying a space in a basket at the entrance of the compound, to serve as an example of the wrath of the master King Leopold.

Could this be what prevents so many hip hop artists from doing what is appropriate for the community? Probably not completely, nonetheless it is a different point of view.

All the following was mentioned to preface an interesting idea. African American women may notice this less, but when a white woman comes in proximity of an African American male, she will immediately grasp, with precision, her belongings. Sometimes they clutch their handbags so tight that one would think that the dye would ooze from its seams.

It is hardly clear how closely this particular phenomenon has been studied, however, it appears that there exists a level of pathological behavior on behalf of white women so severe, that the fallout should be examined under more intense scrutiny. Perhaps the reason the matter has not garnered further attention, is because this asinine behavior has become acceptable. Everyone feels white women should be afraid of African American men. Even more disturbing are the African American women who with excitement and disdain clasp their own handbags to inform African American males that they are being watched. This obsequious gesture, some surmise, is to afford the self-deprecating African American woman an opportunity to move beyond her feelings of inadequacy; this mere event may allow one to feel she is actually bonding with her Caucasian counterpart.

One may question whether any psychopathology has been identified, but why would not a white woman be afraid of an African American male? Especially when one considers that the Caucasian race bought and sold people of African descent for hundreds of years, killed tens of millions in the process, raped children and maimed countless more just to maintain the comfortable lifestyle that most were afforded just because they were white. These individuals went so far as to engage in the delusion that such barbaric behaviors were God's will. In short, psychopathic behaviors, which survived to the detriment of African Americans, continued for hundreds of years.

Does Emmit Teal, ring a bell? More than a phrase in a Kanye West hit, the fourteen-year-old baby, was beaten to death for whistling at a white woman. What about the countless number of lynchings that transpired because a white woman told a lie, that an African American man pursued her, spoke to her, or even looked at her in a manner unbecoming to a "gentile" white woman. Many times it was the white woman whose advances were thwarted.

Lest the world forget apartheid? The Dutch, who themselves felt persecuted in their homeland, The Netherlands, settled in South Africa merely because the weather was suitable to their liking. At that time, the Dutch has no idea of the other natural resources, which blanketed the underground. Mind you, millions of South Africans had to die for this comfort that the Dutch experienced. Moreover, the Dutch eventually raped the countryside and pillaged the natural resources making trillions of dollars in the process, while South Africans were ravaged by disease and incessant poverty. Circumstances, which were manufactured by the Dutch. The Dutch abused South Africans and harbored cheap labor like their Caucasian brethren in America. Even when Dappa Pepple secured a monopoly in the palm oil trade in Africa in the 1800s, the colonials stripped him of this well built business opportunity, and he was forced into exile. Africans were seen as barbarians and unworthy of wealth and comfort.

Now, how can someone who is part of a culture that has been always the aggressor, that massacred, raped, enslaved, be afraid of those whom have been the perpetual victims? It hardly seems likely that a white woman is genuinely afraid of African American men. Instead, it is more realistic, that this is yet another manipulation. One more opportunity to keep the African American male in "his place." White women have been, however, delusional regarding perceptions of African American males. White women, and men, want to be able to justify the racism, which has poisoned America, and the rest of the world. Certain nincompoops wish to believe that the white woman still needs to be protected from the African American male. If one believes one's delusion, one can justify the wretched conditions, which still permeate the African American culture.

One of the biggest problems related to the pervasiveness of negative images associated with the African American community, and particularly males, is the popularity of hip hop. Consider the images being broadcast throughout the world of thugs who kill cops, rob banks and sell drugs on street corners. And the images of females who appear to do little more than dress scantily, talk in a sexually explicit manner, and assume no semblance of appropriate comportment. One could realistically reach the conclusion that African Americans do little of a meaningful nature.

Certainly, children go away feeling and experiencing the deepest impact of negative images. They ultimately imitate and emulate. It used to be that it was hard to hear vulgar language in daytime radio and television; however, as radio stations particularly geared toward African Americans become more liberal these sinister plots are hatched. Plots which enable children who are impressionable, to develop behavior and demonstrate values which undermine African American culture. At the same time, inanely accepted behavior merely affords whites, especially white women, to substantiate their purported fear of African American men. As noted earlier, the fear is more likely delusion, or a tool of manipulation. No one can deny, that hip hop seldom does anything overtly to diminish the ill will of others. Largely, because of those who fail to recognize its ultimate impact on the global culture. Often, one can fail to pursue with vigor, the reason it is alright for certain materials and images to reach African American children, while it is not alright for white kids. Please be advised, that my position, and that of others is that there is no substitute for good parenting; effort which could limit certain breaches. However, one need only look at the helm of any major media network, and overwhelmingly, these positions are held by whites, and occasionally African Americans afraid to do more than nurture the status quo.

Even though rap artists can be arguably some of the most talented people on the planet, they fail to use vast sums of intellect because they have been hoodwinked into thinking that music by African Americans sell more copies the more vulgar and raunchy it is. They have even given it a name "Active Radio Format." To the defense of some hip hop purveyors, not everyone has music laced with explicit sex. Thank goodness for Faith Evans. Artists like Faith are less numbered than those who espouse violence and other derelictions. Be advised that given the state of the current hip hop industry, white women will continue to strangle their handbags at the sight of African American male; even if he is clad in a three piece suit.

LAW: LIARS AND WEASEALS?

To anyone even remotely familiar with the entertainment industry, it rings as no secret that the entire industry is full of lawyers. We hear many jokes about lawyers because there is an apparent disdain for what the public perceives that they represent. Some feel that lawyers are in existence to protect to sanctity of the American justice system, while others believe that lawyers lie and manipulate, which is their sole purpose for existence.

No one can deny that attorneys wield a lot of power. After all, they appear to know all the ins and outs of every situation, and perhaps a way around what appear to be insurmountable obstacles.

Particular names in the entertainment industry, such as Joel Katz, Vernon Slaughter, Alan Grubman, David Indursky, David Ingber, Larry Rudolph, Johnathan Leonard and Kasim Reed are familiar. In fact to some individuals in the field of entertainment these names are the only legal minds of importance.

In my own personal dealings with the entertainment industry, I have come to know individuals who refuse to make a move in the absence of their lawyer. Much like what one could witness with Anna Nicole Smith. In her television show, her attorney Howard Stern refused to leave her side. It was an amusing spectacle, but Anna had grown dependent on Stern. And this was certainly in his best interest. Some people do have attorneys, who act as high priced patsies. Lawyers are of particular interest to me because of the psychological elements that shape the personality of an individual who chooses such a profession. Especially, those who use their skills in unscrupulous ways.

Bar associations across the country weigh in with their spin, that lawyers are purveyors of justice, yada, yada, yada. But why do you suppose that so many people have such disdain for lawyers? Maybe it is because the public has been inundated with reasons to be repulsed by the legal lemurs.

Over the years, my research has revealed some interesting personality traits that are largely shared by certain lawyer types. Primarily, those who seem to engage in unethical behavior and to the extent that the behavior becomes habitual. The resultant behavior may or may not cause a lawyer to be disbarred or a judge to be impeached. Instances do exist wherein a lawyer has failed to complete duties professionally, stolen money from a client, engaged in conflicts of interest, maybe even committed murder.

Antisocial Personality Disorder is a pathological condition for which the main features include manipulation, deceit, and disregard for the welfare and safety of others. For some lawyers there has been a history of consistent behavior for so long that it can be traced back to childhood.

Perhaps there is an unconscious drive for one to choose the profession of law because it masks one's tendency to be manipulative. Maybe the individual does not care to mask deceitful character traits, but simply wishes to allow them to blossom in full regalia without threat of repercussion.

Fancy the power of one who was a lawyer who gets the opportunity to sit in the judge's seat. Cases abound of judges who have been given the supreme authority, only bestowed on precious few to squander the honor. Consider Federal judge Sarah Evans Barker of the U.S. District Court for the Southern District of Indiana. Judge Barker has occupied several positions on boards affiliated with her alma mater, Indiana University. Including her board of director's membership with Clarian Health Partners (Methodist, Indiana University, Riley Hospitals). A Plaintiff filed a lawsuit against Indiana University. The case was heard in Judge Barker's Court. It does not take a juris doctorate to surmise that the appropriate thing to do in this case would be for Judge Barker to recuse herself, however, she in fact ruled in this case. Moreover, she tried to justify her behavior. Judge Barker failed to see how her apparent manipulation failed to overwhelm the general public. I took this matter one step further by providing a survey to children at a junior high school. Even the children came to the conclusion, that in this matter Judge Barker should have recused herself from the case.

U. S. District Judge Alcee Hastings was successfully impeached because he committed perjury and engaged in bribery. In addition, Hastings used confidential information that he obtained in a wiretap to secure his bribes.

The early nineties were plagued with media attention surrounding the brutal murder of Sarah Tokars. Sarah was a bright and beautiful homemaker who happened to be married to a prominent Atlanta attorney and judge, Fred Tokars, who was convicted of orchestrating his wife's murder. Many of Fred Tokars' business associates also received extensive prison sentences for various felonies related to the ultimate demise of Sarah.

Sarah, a homemaker and mother of two was gunned down in front of her two small children. One of the boys had Sarah's brain matter on his clothes when he was found dazed and confused after running to safety. It was discovered that Sarah had uncovered the secret behind some of Fred's business dealings. He was afraid that she would use this information against him in a divorce to gain a larger settlement. In addition, the information could also impact negatively his legal career. The hit man Fred hired was a crack addicted African American male. This derelict was hired by one of Fred's business partners Eddie Lawrence. Fred Tokars, who claimed to defend individuals against injustices, and made rulings as a judge in such matters, had his chronic pathological behavior unmasked in the wake of his inability to control his manipulation, and his need for power and control over others.

Kimberly Anderson, a graduate of Columbia Law, and one who has experienced a lively career in the profession as first General Counsel of Grady Hospital in Atlanta, and then General Counsel for the Atlanta Housing Authority eventually found herself in the position of Executive Director for AID Atlanta, the largest and oldest AIDS service organization in the south. It was in this position that her ultimate character flaws became exposed. As Anderson stood before her staff, including a litany of counselors, social workers, and other helping professionals, she proclaimed that she had illegally accessed medical records from her former employer, Grady Hospital. Furthermore, the information Anderson admitted that she obtained, because she "had connections," was for nothing more profound than she simply wanted the information. Anderson's proclamation was made before the very group of individuals whom are held accountable to the highest degree, for protecting the confidentiality of others. The very arrogance is an obvious feature of a legal professional gone awry.

The code of silence prevents lawyers from divulging the misdeeds of colleagues or speaking publicly regarding their behavioral mishaps. The public's fear of reprisal from a lawyer, and especially a judge keeps most victims from ever reporting heinous acts of legal practitioners. The canons appear to have little influence on the behavior of the legal practitioner with pathological tendencies. This is no surprise, as according to my findings these persons display clear features of Antisocial Personality Disorder, or Sociopathy (psychopath). These types of lawyers have no regard for the law they practice; it is their pawn.

The entertainment industry as a whole encompasses varying degrees of psychopathology. Entertainment is virtually make-believe for the vast majority of the worldwide population. Only a select few are ever privy to the decadent world of entertainment. Very few can ever fathom having their name up in lights, being bombarded with paparazzi, or taking home a multi-million dollar paycheck. Not to mention all the access money and fames offers.

Hip hop is by far one of the most controversial forms of popular entertainment. Especially with its provocative images of gun wielding and exploitation of women. But given the educational level of many of its largest contributors, the hip hop artists are more prone to victimization. On the business side of entertainment, and in the general public, hip hop artists are believed to be dumb and expendable. There are notable exceptions such as Jay Z, Dr. Dre, and Sean "P. Diddy" Combs. This is not to say that all forms of entertainment do not endure stigmatization, however, the negative impressions are more pervasive about the hip hop artists. And hip hop artists contribute to this public opinion.

The entertainment community puts a lot of faith in attorneys, as does much of the world, however, entertainers appear to depend on their lawyer, as if the person is their savior. Possibly because there is so much money at stake. This circumstance puts the lawyer in somewhat of a position of the almighty "Oz". A figure that holds the key to understanding and ruling the entire world. But if lawyers were so very special, why do so many entertainers, especially rappers get involved in so many scandals of their own making? Is it that these people buy into the hype and therefore they feel they have protection from responsibility and reprisal for their actions? Do lawyers encourage such behavior? Why did Kobe Bryant create such a scandal? Did he know he would get out of his trouble?

Take for instance the financial woes of musical phenoms Toni Braxton and TLC. All parties were linked to contracts with LaFace Records. I suppose it never seemed peculiar to most, that both Toni Braxton and TLC filed bankruptcy claims amid being underpaid by LaFace Records. In the case of TLC, the group had a production deal contract with a company owned by the wife of LaFace Records Co-President, Antonio "L.A." Reid.

The lawyers who worked with Braxton and TLC had very close ties to LaFace Records and an allegiance thereto. One must be at least a little curious why attorneys allow their clients to ink certain deals. After all, if one company is so impressed with the talent of a potential superstar, so will someone else be.

My theory is, having some of the attorneys I have over the years, is that attorneys often encourage their clients to engage in self-destructive behavior. First the attorney usually gets paid a considerable sum of money to ward off potential liabilities of a world-class scandal. Far too often the lawyer's psychopathology supercedes any good sense at all. The lawyer may believe in his own invincibility. Lawyers will transfer their feelings of intellectual superiority across all circumstances. Even when indicating that their intentions were not purposeful, the lawyer, may through their training, believe that it is better to lie than to simply own up to one's responsibilities. In some cases long-term inappropriate behavior by a star can be circumvented with the necessary intervention.

Hip hop/r & b star R. Kelly has significant legal troubles. Why would any attorney deny the opportunity to get Kelly the mental health care he desperately needed. Notwithstanding rape or child molestation convictions, it is clear that a problem existed dating to before his romantic involvement with the beautiful and ultra talented hip hop titan Aaliyah. Kelly's behavior should have been addressed years earlier, and even if Kelly would not listen to publicists, managers and friends, the lawyers were in an excellent position to direct Kelly to the appropriate resources. Why would they want to? Lawyers have made a king's ransom defending Kelly and structuring payments to those who were allegedly abused and sexually assaulted by the music impresario.

Many record companies are led by lawyers, including J Records owned by Clive Davis. Masses were unaware that Davis is an attorney, and that his career in entertainment began in the legal department at CBS Records. While the elderly Davis appears to seek harmony in his life, his early career was plagued by legal woes, including a jail sentence as a result of the payola scandal, which forever speckled the landscape of the recording industry.

THE EXPLOITATION OF
B2K

Entertainment over the years has been overrun with stories of all types of stars that are taken advantage of by unscrupulous managers and minions thereof. One of the most tragic cases of exploitation, at least in recent years, has to be there circumstances of B2K.

Of course, my belief is that parents should always be involved in anything that impacts the welfare of a child, if they have the child's best interest at heart. Particularly, they must have the wherewithal to handle the business of their children as well. At a minimum, if the child is an entertainer, the parent should be able to hire the appropriate persons.

Anyone who is familiar with me knows that I am of the notion that children should be protected from predators at all costs. Hollywood and every entertainment sector are full of predators. Predators occupy space in every corner of the universe, but in the entertainment industry there appears to be many more than in the general population. One has but to inquire why it is that the entertainment industry purports entertainers must be progressively younger. The industry continues to snag children who can add to their coffers. I have taken it upon myself to ask entertainment lawyers, and a few record company executives about this phenomenon. The answers generally center on the idea that the child stars have more longevity, and that they appeal to the younger market. Lovely, and well rehearsed answers, but based on my own observations the children are easier to take advantage of. More often than not, their parents tend to know very little about the business of entertainment. Moreover, very few know about the business of business. It is not uncommon that parents of child stars are inept in matters of personal finance, making the child star even more vulnerable.

Frequently, the record companies go after the child stars because they can be exploited in every way, including sexually. This can leave permanent emotional scarring. If the point were for the child star to have longevity the public would see more of them withstand the test of time. Many are signed to record companies whose recording projects are never released. These children may even stay signed to the record company for years. Long enough time for the children to become prey of producers, managers and other label employees.

One should become immediately concerned when adults become completely consumed with someone who is underage, whatever guise one may use to rationalize this unnatural acquaintance. Granted, Chris Stokes is a talented and very ambitious man. And there can be no doubt that he is a producer who can develop music that catches the ear and pockets of the public. Stokes also knows how to select boys who will become teen heartthrobs. Obviously Stokes is a visionary who never wastes time when it comes to exploiting a particular idea or image. From Stokes' public and private history it is clear that he certainly has what appears to be nothing short of magic when he is working with young boys, whether prepubescent or adolescent.

For anyone who does not know Stokes, he brought to public recognition B2K and IMX (formerly known as Immature). B2K is arguably one of the most successful African American boy bands ever conceived. With platinum selling CDs, attached to several world tours, movies and an endless appearance schedule, they were destined to become as big as any boy band could be. However, something in this magnificent conglomerate of adolescent innocence and testosterone unraveled in a dramatic climax. On the other hand Immature, or rather IMX as they are now known still maintain their humble and peculiar association with Stokes. Perhaps because there was less of a public hysteria associated with IMX, which rendered them more controllable. The world may never know. But there were fewer individuals from outside the Stokes wall, coming in contact with IMX as opposed to B2K. The wall was comparable to the Great Wall of China.

Each question to Stokes regarding details of the lives of B2K is answered with another PR spin response. The fact of the matter is that these boys from B2K were perfectly poised for exploitation of varying degrees and origins. Because for the most part, their parents failed to maintain control or manage the lives of their children.

Curious to me, was how any parent would allow a preteen boy to go and live with a stranger, who has no reasonably documented parenting skills. Either desperation and/or neglect by parents can lead to such circumstances. Stokes, while he was not a parent to B2K had a responsibility to act as such when he decided to have these young boys live with him. More incredible is that out of all the adults around Stokes and B2K, including those from the Epic/SONY music label, no one questioned why this grown man wanted to have little boys living with him, who were not his own. Clearly, because of IMX, there was a history of Stokes taking on a pseudo-responsibility with children.

Looking closer, B2K was simply four young boys embarking on adolescence. They were handsome and working in the entertainment industry. While they already attracted attention, they received even more because they were entertainers. Children at this age are particularly vulnerable to peer pressure and parental direction is absolutely necessary. If Stokes were acting as a responsible parent as he claimed, B2K (DeMario, Omarion, Fizz and J Boog) would never have been able to party as if they were adults, going so far as to have young girls spend the night in the apartment the boys shared with Stokes. There are some young ladies who will read this and be very clear of what is meant. In fact, this passage is dedicated to them. Mayhem usually ensues under the circumstances heretofore described.

Stokes is one of only a few who knew his motives, and based upon my observation there are some who obviously had no clue of his intentions early on, but ultimately became overwhelmed with Stokes' sanguine picture of wealth and power. Some will say that any African American boy who is sexually active as a youngster should be admired by adults. Foolishly, there are even females in the African American community who celebrate this ridiculous notion. Some adults, who become sexually engaged with African American children, especially when the children are entertainers, believe that they are not to be chastised because these children are so "mature." The well being of African American children in entertainment is ultimately derailed. Unfortunately, this is what sets the stage for children to be exploited, which was certainly the case with B2K.

Exploitation in the entertainment industry is standard, but this does not make it right. Children certainly lack the intellect and emotional fortitude to deal with matters of exploitation, as do adults. B2K lacked the capacity to understand that the man they lived with, who said he was assuming the role of "surrogate father" was not supposed to be producer, manager, employer and landlord. This would explain why so many issues arose as to just how much money each of the members of B2K was entitled to under the terms of their agreement with Stokes, and Epic/SONY. The only member of the B2K group who was well aware of where he stood financially and contractually was Omarion. This is only because his mother and Stokes were very good friends. An advantage not shared by DeMario, Jboog and Fizz. Unusual huh?

The uphill battle faced by these young men is appalling, but far too familiar. I had an opportunity to visit with the group while they were on one of their tours. It became painfully clear that the record company, nor Stokes could care less about the safety and well being of B2K. At one show there was complete and utter chaos. The young men scaled 15-foot speakers, which were not secure and could have easily tumbled; potentially causing injury or death to B2K, or the fans down below. Representatives from Epic/SONY were present, and my concerns were voiced to the corporate stooges on hand to no avail. Nary a finger was lifted by company representatives to investigate any issues of safety relating to mere kids. This was not all. At the height of pandemonium, no pun intended, and because there was inadequate security, young girls stormed the stage trying to get a piece of B2K.

In one case there was a young girl who was forced into the stage because all of the pushing from fans. Security was forced to lift her onto the stage. The girl was then rushed backstage. Security seemed to feel that there was more pressing concerns because the girl was left unattended and without medical care. But I digress. The Epic/

SONY representatives gazed in delight at the danger and hysteria because the anarchy was evidence of just how much money the company could make from these vulnerable tykes. History has revealed how true this idea would become.

Positively, there existed no one in the Stokes camp who was solely interested in the welfare of B2K, collectively and individually. This would explain why they did not receive sufficient educations. Stokes was certain to strip tutors and teachers of any power. A structure was put in place so that no "responsible" adult would recognize any details of more sinister exploitation. Often adults who were "consultants" (teachers) that were required by the state of California to provide a reasonably standard education for the members of B2K, were completely isolated from the activities of which B2K participated day and night.

State of California regulators in this case, failed to make necessary checks to ensure that these children working in the entertainment industry were receiving their educations. Sadly, many educators in the position of providing education to juvenile performers do not speak up when the system is clearly not functioning properly. Maybe they feel intimidated by producers and managers. Maybe they are in awe of the entrainment environment, and wish to continue working in the same capacity. The money is good. Whatever the reason, B2K got shafted all around and this is unconscionable.

Stokes has always made it clear to those parents who wish to be involved in their child's lives, that he would not be able to work with their children. Of course, this would be frightening to a desperate parent, with limited income and resources, who places his/ her own salvation on the shoulders of their child. Much to the dismay of responsible citizens, the idea is almost unfathomable.

One may ask, are the members of B2K scarred for life? The answer is possibly. Certainly, the young men are forever changed. There is absolutely no way that B2K could have their experiences and not have those experiences shape their personalities for an entire lifetime. Some misguided souls may feel that the exploitation of B2K is a reasonable trade-off for the fame they received in return. I disagree as certain experiences can rob a child of the chance to ever experience a friendship or relationship in an honest and connected way. Eventually, those who have been exploited internalize the outcome as their own fault. They become eternal victims of guilt and shame.

Stokes was not putting together a "family". Each of the now young men, is plagued by the horrible film of their past exploitation that may have surfaced before the advent of B2K, but that certainly flourished in the presence of such a marketing behemoth. Remnants of this manifestation are clear from the arrest of DeMario (Raz B), and is evident in the aggression he has displayed. These behaviors became increasingly evident over the years, and subsequently culminated into fistfights. Manhandling of women was also part of the resultant fallout now and before B2K was disc banned.

Opportunities, even lucrative ones, can continue to present for the forgotten members of B2K. This time they should be much more aware of what lies underneath the fins of the record company shark. Especially, since Epic/SONY was able to hide behind the corporate mask, eluding any responsibility for the abuse B2K endured at the hand of Chris Stokes. This mere demonstration is more proof of just how dispensable companies such as Epic/SONY feel African American artists are. Precisely why negative images of African Americans displayed in hip hop, and the resultant damage is of no consequence to record companies who will find more children to exploit. The entertainers are merely part of the minstrel show. Many are overwhelmed and blinded by the promise of "bling."

HIP HOP BABIES

Have you ever witnessed a child acting older than her years, by putting on makeup, the clothes she wears? Did she provide an adult-like response to a simple question? Did you and others not think it was "cute" for her to do? Well, many share your sentiment. The problem is that certain things are inappropriate at all times. The sad part is that there are some who do not realize the negative implications of some behaviors. This is the dilemma of the hip hop baby.

What is a hip hop baby? The hip hop baby came into existence post 1978. there is an undeniable characteristic of the hip hop baby. Those born of this cohort are mostly African American, most often born of single parent households. Moreover, they are too often the product of teenage mothers.

The surface of the situation may only appear that a tragedy exists with the mother hardly prepared to care for her child emotionally or financially. It would appear that the worst that could transpire is another lifetime recipient of the nation's inadequate welfare system is born.

Since 1978 hip hop has grown exponentially in popularity. Hip hop includes rap music as well. Many radio stations have been developed to specifically host the music genre. And stations that were previously pop have incorporated this electronic, and some-times-forceful description of hard knock values and dismal cultural circumstances.

The hip hop baby is usually apathetic, lazy, and disrespectful and has a total disregard for authority figures. They seldom see the value in hard work. An examination into the average college student, even at HBCUs (Historically Black Colleges and Universities), and this idea is demonstrated perfectly. The African American community has witnessed a surge in teenage pregnancies since 1978. And Planned Parenthood has hardly been effective in curbing the pandemic. (instead young girls have learned how to become sexually active earlier, and in what they deem more effective ways). Girls have found ways to defer the inevitable while engaging in sex until such time the "accident" happens.

Hip hop has exposed children to the glorification of destructive behavior. There have been record companies that have gone so far as to name their companies after alleged behavior, for which the patriarchs were believed to be engaged (i.e. Murder Inc.). "It's harmless fun" some say. But, is it? Women in hip hop are portrayed as "bitches" and "hoes". Some girls even now think it is a good thing to be referred to as such. Everyone knows by now, that many rap videos are going to contain young women, some girls, inappropriately dressed, seen engaging in unflattering behavior. Many young African American girls actually aspire to be video vixens, and jokingly refer to themselves as "video ho wannabes." Even more troubling is that parents increasingly do not see a problem with such pursuits.

Innuendo is virtually non-existent in hip hop. Sex, violence, death and disrespect the blatantly perpetuated and featured in video mediums. Children have begun to experience these concepts early on. By the time parents realize that it is a problem, it is much too late. Parents often feel it is alright for children to watch music videos. It used to be that certain images were not allowed during afternoon hours, and during primetime, when children were likely to see such abhorrent images.

Let's examine the effect that this has on boys. Impressionable and impetuous, without the necessary role models, the television provides images of what are believed to be strong men, who take what they want, how they want it. For this, they are rewarded. Women are merely sex objects. Crime, in the videos, results in flashy cars, jewelry and big houses. Life is a never ending party. All this fame and fortune resulted from very little work. Few realize the long-term impact, and performers are quick to assert that they are not "role models." Parents must be responsible for their own children. A vicious cycle ensues because these children are the products of hip hop babies, and often their parents lack the cognitive intelligence, and social development to understand that the images are destructive to their children. These parents feel this way because after they listened to hip hop, they themselves "turned out alright." Without external markers, it may appear to be true.

Recently, I had the opportunity to attend a party hosted by a platinum selling rapper, and the event was replete with the normal good spirited fun that is always visible at this type of undertaking. The interesting thing was that there were a group of children dancing, who raged from about 4 to 8 years of age. The girls were conspicuously sexually suggestive, even though they probably did not realize the full impact of their behavior. Merely, they were emulating and imitating what they had seen in the music videos, and from their parents. As one mother, in a quite a festive demeanor shouted, from a song by the Ying Yang Twins, "shake it like a salt shaker!" From this point, the other girls began to dance and shake even harder as they were applauded by adults, hence reassured that their behavior was acceptable. There was a young boy present who appeared to be about 5 years of age. A man with platinum front teeth, and drenched in what appeared to be about a million in jewelry bellowed to the young boy, "you better get on it, don't be scared!" The platinum toothed parent was suggesting to the little boy that he should dance suggestively with one of the little girls. The entire scene was completely inappropriate. Me being the person I am supplied the voice of reason. It was obvious given the response to my comments that the adults and parents present felt there was nothing wrong with the manner in which the children interacted. Also, it was apparent that the behavior would have continued, and perhaps escalated if something was not said to the contrary. These same parents, would probably report later, when their daughters are in the throws of adolescence, they cannot understand how the child got pregnant. Nor will they be able to connect the cause of pregnancy and sexual promiscuity to parental encouragement a half dozen years earlier. Or worse, they may not feel there is anything wrong with this either.

Perplexing, is that even the clothes little girls wear are suggestive, such as tight fitting jeans, hip huggers, and low cut shirts. Wording on the clothing, such as "sexy", and "hustler" are occupying a more popular position in children's fashion. Yes, "Hustler". The brand that has become a favorite of college age girls. Unfortunately, the trend has spiraled downward. The problems continue to brew, and there seems to be no one available who recognizes the long-term effects, which linger on the horizon. The difference between the parents of old, and one who is a hip hop baby is that the product of hip hop does not register with the parent as being detrimental to the child.

Years ago African Americans would shield their children from violent and sexually suggestive images, while now, the hip hop baby believes that the images are harmless, and often imperative that their child be exposed to the "real world." However, one must keep in mind, that children are not as emotionally equipped as adults. Therefore, they are incapable of internalizing incoming messages in a healthy way what they experience in the environment, if the input is not in a certain deliverable form. Children are impressionable and they can be nurtured to become highly susceptible to victimization later.

The hip hop baby feels it necessary to thwart authority as opposed to adhere to its boundaries and declarations. This message is passed on to children. Children are more disrespectful to adults, earlier in their lives—many fail to see this as a problem. As a result, the behavior goes uncorrected. Eventually, behavior is out of control, and often there is a parent on the other end, often a single mother purporting that she "did all she could do," and that "I raised my kids to have respect," failing to see all the deficiencies existing. Because at the time she would have been prepared emotionally and intellectually to properly sustain a child, is the time when the child has reached adolescence. This is not meant to be an indictment of all single mothers and fathers. However, it should be a wake-up call that 12 and 13 year olds cannot be expected to raise children properly. Most of the time grandparents would have to take on the responsibility. Usually this task is met with hostility on behalf of the grandparents, and apathy and entitlement on behalf of child bearers.

Power struggles typically ensue, and the child feels unwanted, distant, disconnected and alone.

Bow Wow, the multi-platinum recording artist is one of these hip hop babies. A young man who is a product of the hip hop generation, who has developed a cadre of bad behaviors. In my direct observation of Bow Wow, it has been determined that he has a complete disregard for authority, and especially his mother. This product of hip hop also believes that females are available only for his pleasure. He feels he can treat them however he pleases. Grown women, even before he reached a suitable age were throwing themselves at his feet. Behavior such as this only exacerbates the belief that women and girls are merely objects to be used and discarded. To add insult to injury, older men encourage his inappropriate behavior. The likelihood that adults will ever be truthful with him regarding his ignoble manner is lessened because he is known as the livelihood for so many. Primarily, those who would be in a position to keep his behavior in check. No one can deny that there are normal hormonal changes present in a developing adolescent; however, Bow Wow's behavior is becoming progressively worse with age. Pair an overly active, sexually aggressive, verbally abusive adolescent male with a female, who may or may not have a solid self-concept, and there thrives a recipe for disaster.

Rappers, as well as other youngsters who are in that vulnerable adolescent stage, often are not addressed with the authority necessary to circumvent catastrophic events. Physical and mental care is often warranted. Parents too often want to feel as though everything with their child is under control. Furthermore, a parent feels that a child with a mental health condition is an indictment of the parent.

One can expect that an entire community is in disarray if everyone chooses to remain in denial.

What is a parent to do? Well, it may not be easy, yet it is simple. Parents have to begin to take control of this epidemic by living up to his and her responsibility. This means that parents cannot really be best friends to children. Parents have to make unpopular decisions. Children are resilient and they will get over hurts that are born of their best interest. Maybe it is time that professional help is sought to deal with the emotional strife felt within families. Parents have to begin establishing necessary and appropriate boundaries; maintaining and adhering to standards. Even if a parent feels that they are being hypocritical, it is necessary that children know that it is not okay to disrespect authority, dress provocatively, have risky sex or sex at all before a certain age, and consume drugs and alcohol. Conversely, it is necessary for children to respect parents and elders and to discuss problems children have with their parents. Standards and boundaries help a child to feel safe, and protected. Any responsible parent wants this for their child.

WHY DO THEY ACT THE WAY THEY DO?

EMINEM

It is easy for one to feel that they know all there is to know about Marshall Mathers, a.k.a. Eminem. The Caucasian rapping machine who has almost single handedly landed the hip hop recording industry on its proverbial ear. This self-described lyrical master was discovered by hip hop producer and former NWA rap group member Dr. Dre. Eminem has made for himself, Aftermath (Dr. Dre's record label) and Interscope Records many millions of dollars.

The blockbuster movie Eight Mile was to be loosely based on the life of Eminem. Many interpret that they have the entire story of the life of this iconic rapper. Well, there is a lot the public does not know about Eminem, his family and romantic relationships, than can ever be captured in a book, rap lyrics or a surreptitiously cast Hollywood epic. The movie Eight Mile netted a Grammy and an Oscar, however, it did very little to heal the emotional wounds of the real Marshal Mathers, nor the emotional ills that linger in his marriage, with his daughter, and the torment of which he seeks to hide from each day. And which wears the face of his mother.

The true depth of the heinous acts and catastrophe witnessed by Eminem was glossed over in the movie version of his life, and no song runs as deep as the true mayhem he dealt with from about the age of four. It is not easy for any child to witness someone for whom they deeply love hurt themselves drugs and alcohol. All the while having to endure the neglect that accompanies such behavior. Being that the child is so dependent on the parent or parents, it is difficult to process what appears to be betrayal. Parents who engage in certain types of behavior are not particularly aware of the dangers to which they expose their children. The main problem is that those who share their addictions are the same individuals who can victimize their children. When small children are victimized, either directly or vicariously, they often internalize that it was their fault; seldom are they convinced otherwise.

Children of drug addicts assume responsibility far beyond what is the emotionally reasonable capacity of a youth. These children typically care for the parent, as well as assuming responsibility for cooking, cleaning, paying bills and caring for siblings, as if they themselves were the parent. The emotionally absent parent even begins to depend on the child. This is called "parentification". The parentified child begins to act as if all parties in the household are children, and that the child bears the responsibility of caring for them and protecting them. If something happens, such as if one of the siblings is assaulted by a stranger or otherwise, the parentified child not only feels the pain of a sibling, but they take on the same hurt feelings as if they were the adults. In addition, the pain is compounded by the guilt they feel for not being able to prevent an attack or circumstance over which they had no control, nor physical strength.

A child in this predicament grows confused by loving and hating the parent equally. These feelings arise because at a certain emotional place the child can intellectualize that they should not be in the parentified position. The child resents the parent because the child has felt compelled to assume the role that was to be reserved for the parent.

People who listen to the news are familiar with the fact that Eminem does not appear to hold his mother in high regard. Moreover, he continues to have a tempestuous relationship with his wife. My belief is that in an effort to take control for past emotional torment, Eminem selected the wife he did because of the similarities between she and his mother. Because the wife and mother were so similar is the reason Eminem exacted to much punishment upon his wife. Eminem had control over this punishment with one twist. A child was produced and he was able to save her from some of the anguish he experienced in his earlier years. Eminem's efforts to protect his daughter, has provided him with at least some catharsis for his own pain, even though he was unaware of the emotional architecture he created. Addressing the source of pain and anguish is very difficult for most, usually substitutes are found (hence, Eminem's wife). Until the cause of his pain is dealt with effectively, his emotions will likely be released in negative ways, violence, and in some positive ways, his therapeutic treatment will appear as lyrical renditions of past experience. Maybe there is a 9 Mile on the horizon.

LIL' KIM

Kimberly Jones, known as rap vixen and sex siren Lil' Kim, was raised in the mean streets of Brooklyn. Lil' Kim rose to become one of the best rappers of all time. An icon that will indelibly go down in history. Any hip hop artist will attest, that having this powerhouse rap a few bars on their tunes, and this is certain to secure a platinum selling project, and a spot on the music charts.

Lil' Kim actually started out performing in gymnasiums and clubs much like every other up and coming performer. During this time Kim learned the poison of the mean streets has a life changing effect. Kim will not deny that she was friends with those individuals who made their lives selling crack cocaine to drug addicts. In fact, some even created crack addicts out of children. Many of these "dealers" were also in the business of orchestrating their own brand of justice. Kim was certainly willing to go along for the "ride."

Admittedly, Kim states that she was a difficult child and refused to listen to authority figures, including her father. Kim's father is credited with rearing her, as her mother was conspicuously absent after the couple divorced. Kim met some people whom she was convinced were her friends. One of the problems with adolescence is that kids at this period tend to look to their peers for guidance and support instead of their parents. Children, who are without appropriate parental interest, are in a more precarious position. In many cases, the parent can provide the child with a foundation that prohibits the child from venturing too far outside of the prescribed behavioral parameters. Kim faced a life changing tragedy, which renders her completely unreceptive to guidance from authority figures. Even Kim did not recognize this at the time that she experienced her life-changing episode. For a time Kim was emotionally isolated from everyone. Today she is a little more receptive but she appears to be unaware that her emotionally vacant feelings, and resultant behavior extends back to her childhood. The anxiety that was formed during her adolescent development is likely responsible for what appears to some, her apparent fixation with changing her appearance, or Body Dysmorphic Disorder (BDD). BDD is a condition wherein a person has an imagined defect in a body part, when in fact, the individual looks quite normal, even incredible according to societal standards. The person with BDD, if one can afford plastic surgery, will begin to engage in the activity, usually concentrating on one body part to "fix." If the condition continues, the individual has the opportunity to concentrate on their other body parts. It is believed that the person with BDD has experienced prior circumstances that have been locked in the unconscious, and this is because having to deal with the situation is too difficult. As a result, because a thought brought to consciousness would be too difficult to deal with, the unconscious causes the individual to focus on a body part.

Young girls on the "outs" with their parents become perfect prey for older predators, who will fill a young girl's head with thoughts of romance and promises of a special future that never materialize. Because Kim always looked younger than her years, and her stature is small, she was approached by a great many men who found her naiveté appealing. From my perspective it is extremely important to maintain a clear accounting of a child's whereabouts, even when the parent feels they are not getting along well with the child. Being a parent is tough, and this means that children will sometimes be mad. They'll get over it. A parent can never stop espousing the necessity for children to understand that parents' rules have to be the supreme foundation of a household.

Ultimately Kim was linked with Notorious B.I.G. with whom she was said to have been romantically involved, and Sean "P. Diddy" Combs, the music mogul who produced the CD, which would make Lil' Kim known throughout the land. While history was made, the demons of her younger days still remain.

50 CENT

Undoubtedly, one of the most popular rap artists to date is Curtis Jackson, a.k.a. 50 Cent, son of the late Sabrina Jackson. 50 Cent appears to be equally layered with talent and Teflon. Among the ladies 50 Cent is considered a preeminent heartthrob. However, many simply wonder why he really never emotionally connects with any of them. Fathering a child and setting up house is one thing, sharing one's innermost secrets, desires, aspiration and pain is quite another.

The abrasive exterior of 50 Cent that most have come to know is only outweighed by his personal torment, which predates his adolescence. The death of Sabrina Jackson created a very difficult emotional roadmap for the star. 50 Cent effectively avoids discussing in any detail, his personal anguish over the loss. After the death of Sabrina, 50 had grandparents who were willing to care for him. However, their own feelings of grief and loss robbed them of the ability to care for 50's depression. Part of the grief process is denial. 50 has been in the denial stage of grief since the death of his mother. No one close to him ever recognized that he was in denial because he was such a strong boy, at least on the outside. It was believed that 50 was handling the demise of Sabrina very well under the circumstances.

The behavioral problems in 50's preadolescence and adolescence was merely a conscious manifestation of his unconscious denial. He was simply lashing out, mostly because of the anger towards himself of which he was consciously unaware.

The clincher is that on the surface it appeared that 50 was just a "kid gone bad," when in actuality he became involved in certain situations because he had a "death wish." His behavior had progressed to the point that he was suicidal even though he consciously had no conception.

As those close to 50 can recall, and that he himself will attest, there were times when he engaged in behaviors that seemed brazen and heroic, stupid and unnecessary. There were some behaviors that clearly could have led to his death. Engaging to such a degree certainly provided 50 with the reputation that he was fearless, and that he did not care if he died. In fact, my belief is that he hoped he would expire-at least to some degree he would have some control over his life. This is not unusual for the individual with suicidal ideation; they often feel they are better off dead. Hopefully, 50 will ultimately recognize that the demons taunting him daily are keeping him from ever connecting with anyone including his son, whom he unwittingly is turning into a "soldier."

T.I.

Controversy has never had a more conspicuous beacon than rap master, and newly ordained music mogul, T.I. (Clifford Harris) of Atlanta. Raised in the mean streets of northwest Atlanta, T.I. was initiated by the streets by becoming well aware of fighting and jockeying for street credibility. As some know, the fastest and most significant means of establishing street credibility is to engage in drug dealing. Maintaining the credibility requires ruthless behavior. Perfect examples are Irv Gotti of Murder, Inc., Suge Knight of Death Row Records and fortunately to a lesser degree, Jay-Z.

T.I. has only experienced what many African American males have endured of similar backgrounds. What happens is that the direction from home appears to be far less than adequate. Especially in these environments the child becomes parentified. Children like this come from broken and dysfunctional homes far too often. The only direction or guidance is gleaned from inappropriate sources. Once children have been void of necessary parental guidance and attention they are less likely to listen to authority figures at any point later in life. Authority is disregarded as important.

The problems with T.I. were compounded on two fronts. The first was that even after he discovered what a musical talent he was, T.I. continued to engage in his old behavior, which continued to land him in trouble with the law. Second, T.I. believed the "hype" that he had to maintain his street credibility in order to become a rap star. It is important to recognize that he can change his behavior and know what it is to be truly great, not just a rap star. This new notation will not preclude him from being rich. As an up-and-coming rap music mogul, it will be of necessity that T.I. employ his brain over his brawn. T.I. should take to heart that anyone who encourages this publicly proclaimed lyrical mastermind to embrace crime and scandal should be immediately banished from the fold.

JAY-Z

Shawn Carter is a phenomenal businessman, and he is to be commended along with Kareem Burke and Damon Dash for erecting the hugely successful Roc-A-Fella Records and the Roc-A-Wear clothing line, that has become the staple of worldwide urban wear.

Shawn Carter, a.k.a. Jay-Z has had a past riddled with criminal activity, which included violence of various sorts. Assault, attempted murder and drug dealing were all recreation of perpetual pursuit for the aspiring delinquent turned rapper. A lot of Jay-Z's criminal past escaped scrutiny because while he was a street hustler, he was never considered very good at it by his cohorts. Perhaps as part of the media hype related to thug rappers, the publicity machine opted to keep certain items out of his biography, being that he was not deemed a good enough thug.

The youngest of four children reared by a single mother, Jay-Z felt the only means of escaping poverty, and not necessarily the ghetto, was to sell illegal drugs and allegedly commit minor robberies. Jay-Z has a history of running away from difficult situations. This is an escapism because it appears that Jay-Z has difficulties with confrontation when it is expected in reasonable fashion. Personal observations cause me to conclude, that Jay-Z has anxiety, which extends beyond the stage. In fact, he is much more comfortable on-stage because he is not intimately socially accountable to any one person. Jay-Z is apprehensive about speaking to and communicating with people in settings not under his complete control.

Jay-Z's youth was doused with difficulty at home and school, however, he viewed this period as arduous at best. In fact a little concerted effort and guidance from the necessary sources could have prevented the morality breach he experienced. Namely, the young girls whose lives were negatively impacted at the hands of this now beloved musical master. The best part of all this is his public withdrawal, and the anxiety he experiences which could stem from his fear of being found out. Some say that there is talk of guilt and shame associated with the destruction of lives for which Jay-Z may in whole or part feel responsible. What this means is that Jay-Z can be rehabilitated, though this has not yet transpired.

One other item is that Jay-Z appears to value females very little. Since many women were fighting to be near him for a cadre of reasons, some of his idiosyncrasies were never publicized. It is believed, that as part of the escapism mentioned earlier, some of his negative thoughts about females were masked. For someone with Jay-Z's emotional make-up, he would seek the ultimate form of emotional escape. Jay-Z's conquest will be likely a mate who comes from a background completely opposite his own. Even if Jay-Z began to date someone who was also working in entertainment, or if she were a superstar, her family structure and values would be completely opposite Jay-Z's. The problem exists when someone like Jay-Z realizes that they are unable to live vicariously through the childhood memories of someone else. If Jay-Z does not seek to correct past ills that remain a foundation of his self reflection, his behavior in the type of relationship described would change as certain as his birth name is Shawn Corey Carter.

SNOOP DOGG

Calvin Broadus a.k.a. Snoop Dogg was one of those rappers who really bought into the "hype" about gangsta rap. He actually believed that those in the rest of the world (outside of Long Beach, CA) were enthralled by the prospect of gun toting thugs who shoot-to-kill police officers and defile and annihilate their neighbors.

Early in Snoop's career he was plagued by various charges including being implicated in a drive-by shooting. Of course, he was cleared of all charges, but the crowd of people who helped to get Snoop into the mess continued to hang around. Armed with a record company publicist Snoop decided to change his image, as the public's outrage over gangsta rap continued. This is what many derelicts do when they are the field of entertainment. They have exhibited, even flaunted unacceptable behavior. These dregs of society are taught to spin the public instead of changing the behavior. Spinning is only a temporary solution, and ultimately only lands money in the hands of public relations companies and the record companies. What does the company care when they are dealing with an expendable African American?

Mostly raised by his mother, Snoop was one of those children who was by all accounts, neglected. Not that it was his mother's intent, but with her limited resources and abilities, she was unable to provide tools, which would override peer suggestions made to Snoop. Snoop's behavior as a youngster was often inappropriate, and there were numerous complaints from young girls who felt that they were victimized by Snoop's unruly behavior. Police in Long Beach came to know Snoop as a teenager because of his gang associations. But concern mounted as Snoop approached adulthood. Sounds like a familiar story? This simply illustrates my point that the culture can be pervasive. Snoop, like many others, was raised in what was considered "the hood" and those adults with limited skills fail to feel that they are equipped to deal with children who offer resistance. My belief is that many of the parents deal with such a child by using neglect as a tactic. This amounts to lazy parenting.

Reports have surfaced over the years that Snoop is completely devoid of respect for women. This appears to be a pervasive theme amongst many young rappers, and otherwise. Is this because they have not, or feel they have not been apprised of an appropriate image by their own mothers? Upon closer examination, would we see that these men do not respect their own mothers, but rather they control them too? Clearly, it may be that Snoop's music videos are an extension of his personality. It has been reported that throughout his life, interactions with women yield incidents of physical, and other types of abuse. Some have been able to be settled quietly apparently, while others have permeated the marijuana smoke of Snoopville. A bona fide spectacle, Snoop has been questioned regarding the rape of one of his make-up artists. Not to say that he is *really* a rapist, but time will only tell if this latest event is simply an extension of past behavior dating back to about the age of ten.

Children are to be protected from certain images, and they are to be shielded from unnecessary responsibility, which causes them to have to act in adult fashion. Snoop has had a significant influence on Bow Wow, which could likely be the cause of some of Bow Wow's inane behaviors towards his mother and other females.

MAKING MONEY DOESN'T ALWAYS MAKE IT BETTER

Adjustment Disorder is probably what many would think that it is; a condition in which an individual has difficulty adjusting to some experience or set of experiences. It can be a significant event or set of events. What is fascinating about this particular disorder, is that so many feel that the event(s) in question must be negative, and this is simply not so. In my experience, numerous clients have come to me with Adjustment Disorder whom have experienced the most magnificent of occasions. Even something such as earning a multi-million dollar contract to play basketball.

Significant emotional or behavioral symptoms to an identifiable event(s) is essential. According to the DSM IV (Diagnostic and Statistical Manual of Psychiatric Disorders) the symptoms must appear within three months after the appearance of the event in question. Further, the clinical significance of the reaction is indicated by distress, that is significantly greater than what would be expected given the kind of event, or by a significant impairment in social or occupational functioning.

There are numerous stressors, which can cause Adjustment Disorder, most commonly, one tends to associate Adjustment Disorder with the end of a romantic relationship, friendship, or financial difficulties. With children especially, it can be a reaction to a divorce and dealing with the impending or perceived separation from a parent. Usually, the symptoms persist for no more than six months. However, symptoms can continue on longer if the individual faces a prolonged or repeating crisis, or if one is faced with dealing with ongoing issues related to the original event.

For celebrities Adjustment Disorder can be a most peculiar phenomenon for the individual experiencing it because, they themselves are usually wondering "what's going on?" Many celebs feel that they are supposed to be happy because they have received that huge basketball or recording contract, starring role in a film, or that unprecedented modeling contract.

Let us examine some of the other dynamics that can go along with fame and fortune. Most of us do not realize it, but in fact, we could almost all be considered very private individuals. Imagine the change one goes through when paparazzi begin to camp outside the door, and to even venture to the supermarket, security must be conspicuously present. While some celebrities are able to maintain a semblance of normalcy surrounding their lives, even they have to experience the shock of everyone knowing who they are. And there is an increased expectation placed upon them that the general public could avoid. If most of us go out shopping in less than presentable dress, sans make-up, no one would really care, but for an actor who earns $15,000,000 per movie, every newspaper, tabloid and TV magazine is willing to cover the story, with bizarre stories of sickness and drug abuse, whether or not there is any truth to it.

Notoriety in the beginning may seem manageable because the celebrity feels that only the "good things" will be printed and scrutinized, and this is not to mention that all past exploits and indiscretions that tend to magically appear when one achieves celebrity. And if this is not stressful enough, the histories of all family members and close friends anchor under a microscope for the media and the rest of the world to consume.

There are a litany of features that may be recognizable. One may appear sad or depressed and exhibit some signs of depression, while others may appear anxious, or a combination of the above. Recall if any of the following appears familiar, with descriptions of other features which includes the violations of the rights of others, such as ignoring fiduciary responsibilities, reckless driving, fighting, physical abuse, etcetera. This is not to say, that every case of physical assault involving a celebrity is due to Adjustment Disorder, but there are definitely those experiencing the condition who are completely unaware. They tend to act out inappropriately not understanding how to deal with the feelings they harbor so intently. It is important to note, that often there is a mixture of mood and conduct that causes one to experience anxiety and depression, and to act out negatively. African Americans, and those of juvenile chronology are more susceptible to this condition upon gaining fame and fortune.

Physical manifestations can be but one more characteristic of Adjustment Disorder and this can include some complaints of aches and pains, and fatigue. Social withdrawal is another common feature. One may tend to completely pull away from social events and activities for a period of time. I have had some cases in my practice where one was a "social butterfly" and attended every event from house parties to nightclubs, fundraisers to Grammys®, and when she suddenly had a platinum selling album, her picture on magazine covers and offers to appear on virtually every television show around the globe, she began to pull away from social events-the relationships she had with family and friends became stormy and her behavior towards them abusive. A few months of counseling resulted in the client being able to identify what the real issue was. Soon she began to revisit social activities, promote her new album and repair and rebuild relationships with family and friends.

One of my patients is a professional basketball player. The gentleman received a whopping multi-million dollar contract. He had been playing college basketball having received a basketball scholarship at a major university. His grades were good, and he pursued the basketball scholarship not to go to the NBA, but merely to land a job good enough to move his grandmother, mother and siblings out of the worst housing projects in the city where he was born and raised.

My client only dreamed of one day moving into a nice comfortable home and helping some of his brothers and sisters go to college. He was an excellent basketball player and landed a multi-year contract. He became a millionaire overnight, and that comfortable home in the suburbs that he dreamed about became a multimillion-dollar castle surrounded by acres of land, and expensive cars for every family member old enough to drive.

The contention here is not that everyone who was ever poor cannot adjust to living the life of Riley without compunction, but that the privileges do come with a price, for you see what my client learned, was that there was more to owning a large estate, than simply paying the mortgage. Previously having no management experience, he was now in charge of having and maintaining a staff, which could care for a huge home and many acres of property. Cooks, maids, a butler and chauffeur were part of the package. And though he knew somehow he could afford the luxuries, he became stressed trying to comprehend all of his monthly expenses, and the need for such accessories of posh living. His expenses were tens of thousands per month and he explained that he could not help but fear the possibility of ending up back in the housing projects as the months went by. The situation got to a point where he was afraid to look at bills, balance a personal checkbook, or speak to the accountant for fear of what he might discover. No longer would he commiserate with friends in a social setting, and he only attended public functions when told that he had to for contractual reasons. Often he complained of illnesses that kept him at home.

Needless to say, while his expenses were commensurate with what was normal for his home, and the size of his family, he received many times per month in income more than his cash outlay. After several sessions this client was on his way to discovering a more normal existence, and after a significant time of living with his contract he was finally nicely adjusted to wealth and fame. It was important for him to in fact put into perspective his true financial status, and what would still be considered appropriate expenses. The client stated that he "hated" living in the "projects" and that he never wanted to go back. It was necessary for him to see that his fears about "going broke" were completely unwarranted under the circumstances. The feelings of nervousness and worry subsided after several months with on-going counseling.

African Americans in the general population, often, do not seek formal counseling for emotional ailments, so it is easy for matters to grow out of control. In extreme circumstances one may be prompted to visit a pastor, however, sometimes, religious dogma may prevent one from disclosing all the underlying dynamics shaping behavior and turmoil. And the younger the emotional sufferer, the more likely aggression and violence will be displayed.

POP DIVA TAKES A DIVE

One may ask, what is it that would make someone as famous and as sought after Whitney Houston became entangled in the hip hop web? Not that every element of hip hop is negative but her preference, along with that of her husband Bobby Brown, has centered on the portion of hip hop that includes substance abuse, inappropriate child rearing practices, a total disrespect for rules and authority, as well as self-hatred.

There are many who would want to blame the apparent downfall of Whitney Houston on her husband. Bobby Brown was obviously no stranger to the streets, however, he hardly deserves all the credit for the architecture of her demise.

Important to remember is that Houston began her superstar trek at a very early age, and had a full-time job as a performer by the age of 11. While this can be considered a dream come true, it does present major complications as it relates to a youngster understanding her position in society and in her own household.

Children who work and contribute to the household bottom-line are prone to grow up fast, as they are by default enabled to take on a position of control within the household. The more they contribute financially, the more important they become as a decision maker. Parents do not readily realize it, but gradually the child gains more power, and the boundaries, if any were previously established, begin to disappear.

Eventually parents see children less like children and the child sees herself, or at least perceives herself as occupying an adult role. The same rings true for stars like Lindsay Lohan, Hillary Duff, Bow Wow, Mary Kate and Ashly Olsen. What we know about the psychology of a child, at least in most cases, is that if she does not have a chance to experience childhood when it is appropriate, an emotional fixation occurs. Ultimately the behaviors that should have appeared during childhood cease, and the individual most often will experience the manifestation of these behaviors sometime later in life. Often at the most inconvenient times.

There exists a period of vulnerability and susceptibility between the time of age appropriate behavioral manifestations and actual onset of delayed manifestations.

The hip hop generation is very carefree and rebellious. It can too be dog-eat-dog. Most of hip hop is an outpouring of aggression and anger that seeks to justify and in some cases mask a disdain for authority, yet it is disseminated as entertainment. Never mind that impressionable children are listening. To someone who is vulnerable the hip hop mentality is very inviting and empowering. One who subscribes to it and loves it never has to worry about exhibiting appropriate behavior. One never has to be responsible.

A huge question that looms as it relates to why teenagers have become consumed by hip hop, relates specifically to the nature of adolescence. It is described by psychologists as a period of "storm and stress." A tumultuous period wherein the child is struggling to find her own identity. And to understand her emotions. Teenagers are known for their rebellious nature and are notoriously prone to the influence of peers.

Hip hop has a certain raw strength about it. Also, while there are obviously artistic elements involved it is amazing that males and females alike feel beguiled into calling themselves "thugs". Most of us cannot imagine wearing such a name as a badge of honor. How does this connect to Whitney Houston? One Houston captured a full-time job, or rather once it captured her, the child's life took on a power and direction of its own. The childhood became displaced by constant stints in the studio, and countless auditions. All of this was in an effort to secure for Houston the ultimate record deal, which would catapult her to superstardom. Of course, Houston's parents were likely doing what they felt was best; not allowing Houston's significant talent to go to waste.

Years of directed vigilance had finally paid off (some would say) in the form of the fateful meeting with the legendary Clive Davis. Davis was immediately smitten with the personality, style, talent and beauty of the indomitable Houston. Davis saw that this girl could use the intense and provocative leadership of the lawyer turned music man. This was one more opportunity for the adolescent and child emotions to stay trapped within the displaced psyche of a deferred child.

Once Davis had completely taken control of Houston, through the express permission of her parents, the whirlwind began as legions of courtiers were called in to assist in the development of a new superstar. Being created at the behest of Davis, much like the Bride of Frankenstein, Houston the star was molded. Already highly impressionable, when the courtiers were in place, there was no need for Houston to so much as think for herself. On the outside it appeared that she had amassed a great deal of power. Actually, Houston was in a position of complete powerlessness. Clive Davis was the mastermind and the only real power in the game of high stakes that consumed Houston.

Matters of emotions continued to grow worse. Houston went from a child acting as an adult, to an adult being treated as a child. A frustrating situation was unfolding exponentially.

While Houston has a series of high profile romances, it was obvious that they all seemed to share a common trait. Mike Tyson, Eddie Murphy were the most visible. Then came Bobby Brown, the R & B bad boy whose reputation was the talk of tabloids, TV magazines, news reports, barbershops and front porches across the land. Brown was brash, vain and engaged in whatever he fancied with reckless abandon.

Brown possessed a certain power, or at least it seemed. Not caring what anyone thought about him, he regularly engaged in bar room type brawls. Brown had a primitive drive for excitement, like some urban Tarzan, eager to solidify his position at the top of the heap. Houston was eager to align herself with some form of power from which she could emotionally benefit. Something absent from the grasp of Clive Davis. The union if Houston and Brown was sealed.

Gradually, Houston began to live vicariously through Brown. She enjoyed the manner in which he thumbed his nose at the rest of the world. There were plenty of drugs and booze, however, Houston had began her experimentations before becoming attached to Brown. Brown was instrumental in one way by assisting Houston with her assertiveness as it related to her business pursuits, which were those involving Clive Davis. Davis always describes what he did with Houston was simply guide her career, and that everything was carried out with Houston's best interest in mind. Houston eventually vocalized that Davis was trying to control the essential elements of her life.

Obviously, Davis overlooked the dynamics that were part of Houston's life before he entered the picture. Before her fast track to stardom culminated under Davis' tutelage. At some point Houston began to rebel against the most significant authority figure in her life, Davis. Houston had unwittingly transferred her feelings towards her parents to Davis-he had essentially taken on the parental role.

Interventions did occur on Houston's behalf, which were designed to curb some of the behavior with which she was now entrenched. But at this point Houston was more apt to resist in a more aggressive manner. Becoming more enveloped in what she describes as her "experimentation" with drugs, rebellion against authority figures, delayed adolescence; tensions began to heighten between Houston and Clive Davis.

The problem with the union of Brown and Houston was that their histories of emotional struggles, of which those around were not astute, made them bad for each other at that particular time in their lives. Brown was also the product of an environment where he experienced too much too soon. Brown has had childhood experiences, which still have a grip on his psyche.

Negative behaviors on behalf of Houston continued to flourish amid tensions with her record company and her parents. Certain behaviors were escalating even while she was pregnant with Bobby Christina. As Houston began to exert power, she learned how little control she had in the Davis camp. Therefore, Houston became increasingly frustrated. Davis was unsure just how much longer Houston would remain an asset to the Arista Records franchise.

Fighting between Houston and Brown had always existed, however, with Houston's continued consumption of drugs she became more willing to engage in altercations of every kind. The behaviors Houston was displaying appeared more and more like that of a younger person. Houston became embraced by the hip hop culture. The public began to see Houston as "down" and "real", terms pervasively used in the African American community to describe that a person is representative of, and true to what is perceived to be African American culture. This acceptance felt good to Houston. Much like young children who are accepted into brutal gangs. Little did Houston recognize that it was more of a conquest by those around her to have the great pop diva shrouded in scandal and unable to soberly handle her own basic affairs. Houston had been a pop princess, and in the mind of the hip hop power structure, an African American should never seek to occupy such a title, as this is somehow a degradation of African Americans. The hip hoppers feel that this status means that a star who achieved what Houston had meant that she was "being white." This is one of the reasons Ashanti has maintained her position in the hip hop jungle, Murder, Inc.

The more immersed Houston became, the more difficult it became for her to find her healthy emotional foundation. At a certain point she was no longer willing to tolerate the opines of family. When her parents intervened as a result of their concern for Bobby Christina, Houston threatened to flee the country with her man and child in tow. Houston said that if she were pressured she would remain in a self-imposed exile. The grandparents would be deprived of the companionship of their precious granddaughter.

The new millennium ushered in a complete dissention into the abyss of drugs, marital discourse, and professional disappointments.

Houston's record sells were far less than that expected of a pop diva. Matters only became worse as the only people available to assist Houston were drug-abusing hip hop hangers on; those eager to join in Houston's diabolical self-destruction. Surely, there was no shortage of "yes" people whose echololic behavior would continue as long as rocks and drug powder were in the air. Houston's fortune was dissipating as faster than a crack cocaine high.

Apparently, all has not been completely lost, there were still some former courtiers who were still emblazoned with Houston's potential for success. Moreover, Houston still has a friendship with Sean "P. Diddy" Combs and the entire Murder, Inc. family. Some believe that these associations are no good to someone who had achieved the level of fame attained by Houston.

Houston is reported to have tried a variety of therapies to help her stay off of drugs. However, many therapists bow to the pressure of providing services to stars of Houston's stature, which makes so many ineffectual. Many individuals with the power to assist Houston are simply overcome by the star factor, or they are victims of their own countertransference. For some of the therapists they themselves wanted to be recognized as a star. Once a star enters their domain, they do not wish to give up the status so the star, such as Houston begins to set the tone for the therapy sessions, and the therapist is no longer a facilitator and boundary setter. In this description, setting boundaries for a star in Houston's situation will likely mean a therapist falling out of favor with the star. Hence, she may not be ready for treatment; the effort was likely related to spin control.

Though they have not taken as much of a dive in their professional and personal lives, Janet Jackson, Mariah Carey and Britney

Spears were wrought with dilemmas after associating themselves more intimately with the hip hop community. Not just because they performed the music, but because they wanted to live the lifestyle. The transition is easy to make, very difficult from which to recover. In contrast, Jennifer Lopez and Madonna have remained vigilant regarding their image. Haven ridden the fence between pop and hip hop, they are certain to not publicly embrace the hip hop lifestyle as their main choice of lifestyle.

R. KELLY: PRODIGY OR PEDOPHILE?

Robert Kelly, a.k.a. R. Kelly, is without a doubt, a great musical mind. And some would even argue, that he uses significant musical ability to gain simple liberties that are believed to be sacred. Those that most others would not dare to possess. Namely, sexual intercourse with children.

Recent history has been flooded with news reports of high profile people who betray the sanctity of a child's innocence by engaging in heinous acts with them. The more frightening element in all of this is that parents often place their children in precarious positions that could potentially cause them irreparable harm. If a celebrity is in the picture, the parent is more likely to allow contact with a sex fiend, or pedophile (a person who has a sexual attraction to children).

A pedophile is described by the DSM IV (Diagnostic and Statistical Manual of Mental Disorders) as a condition in which an adult has an affinity towards children. The orgin of which is sexual. The pedophile is obsessed with her/his object of desire. The pedophile prefers children who are usually younger than 13 years old. The pedophile can be still attracted to adults, so this frightful condition can go masked indefinitely. It is not uncommon for someone who likes children in such a manner to be married, with children of her/his own.

The pedophile may or may not exert force to engage in sexual activity with a child, and often the pedophile will rationalize their behavior by indicating that the child was somehow seductive and wanted to be seduced by the predatory personality. Hence, the child is scarred for an emotional eternity. And if the pedophile can conceive in his mind that the child has engaged previously in sexual activity, this will only exacerbate the arrogance and disregard for the child's welfare, which is channeled by the pedophile.

Another disturbing element exists in all of this, which is that someone with more power, popularity can be more insidious and elusive to authorities. R. Kelly for instance, has a lot of fans and even though millions of people knew that he engaged in sexual activity with a little girl, that somehow the escapade was justified. This little girl, the one that is on the videotape, which caused R. Kelly to be charged with a crime, and who has faced severe scrutiny from authorities, has become a pariah in the eyes of R. Kelly and the rest of the world. Especially by fans of R. Kelly who obviously feel that is it somehow permissible for grown men to be engaged sexually with children.

This problem is actually all around us. Every adult male who has ever engaged in sex with a teenage girl, a girl who is not of college age, justifies such occurrences by blaming the girl. And in the African American community, so many men have fathered children with girls, that this phenomenon has become acceptable. More bizarre is that parents are no longer vigorous in the defense of their boys and girls. Planned parenthood produced a commercial many years ago, which was one of my favorites. The commercial featured the back of a female putting on makeup in the mirror. As the camera pans to the face one can see that it is a little girl, and a voice bellows "pick on someone your own age." What happened to this campaign? The message apparently has become lost. The people who justify sex with kids are quick to feel an affinity towards those who justify rape.

If a female as a teenager is sexually active, or has been, it does not change the fact that a child is still a child. People who are attracted to children sexually use this idea as an excuse to engage in the inappropriate. No child is ever physically or emotionally prepared to engage in a meaningful sexual relationship with an adult. In these situations the adult is always the one who is in control, and it is impossible for there to be an equitable relationship. No matter how "mature" the child appears to be, the child is still a child. Child sex lovers often use such excuses to justify their behavior, and there is positively no other way in which to state it. The matter is completely unacceptable. So parents, when a 26yo male has sex with your 15-year-old daughter, and even if the girl does not become pregnant, REPORT IT TO THE AUTHORITIES. Young men can also be taken advantage of. Young men are victims too, except often this type of abuse goes unreported. The socialization of men is different, even today with all of the world's education and technology. Predators can be just as dangerous for males. Consider some of the cases, which have entered the news about female teachers who engage in sex with small children.

Males in their masculine stupidity often tell their boys that it is a good thing to engage in sexual activity in their early years, and sometimes pre-adolescent years. This is why many young boys feel that they are supposed to indulge. For many, even the father may hint that he thinks the boy is a "sissy" if he does not engage in sex with a female early on. Somehow this is interpreted by some misguided parents, and others, that there is something wrong with a boy who does not want to have sex with a female before he is of reasonable years. Boys rarely report their victimization by adults. These boys have been conditioned to believe that they have done a "manly" thing by engaging in sex with an adult.

In the case of Mary Kay Latourneau, had she not been caught by police the matter likely would not have been found out, until the boy who fathered her children was an adult. Though it is believed pedophilia involves more male predators than females, my accompanying belief is that socialization of males prevents more acknowledgements of abuse by adults. In the hip hop generation, a young boy may be applauded if he has sex with an adult female.

Consider the case of Usher Raymond. In good faith Johnetta Patton released her son to Sean "P. Diddy" Combs to be prepared for stardom. Sean was to produce a CD for Usher and this would take constant work. At least this is what Johnetta was led to believe. She was also coaxed by Antonio "L.A." Reid, who was at the time one half of LaFace Records. What Usher became faced with was a barrage of non-stop parties, which included drugs, alcohol and sex. Of course, who would expect Combs to have parenting skills, at least at the time in question?

Even though Combs was an adult at the time, he saw the young boy, Usher, as an equal in so many ways. Combs' minions had the same belief so the young Usher witnessed and experienced things that a young boy of his years should not be exposed.

Usher is quick to play it cool about the past, however, the outward signs are quite visible. Usher was in some way victimized by his exposure to Combs' life. On some levels Usher is in denial regarding the impact of the experience. And other parts of this façade are simply public relations damage control. While Usher became a huge star, it is largely due to the fact that ties were severed with Combs, and Johnetta once again assumed custody, responsibility and control of her child.

Be advised, that when an adult is desperate to get his/her hands on your child, and fails to include the parent in activities and plans, one must be especially cautious. One hardly has to be a patron of hip hop to get this message. Children all over, including those in the entertainment industry continue to be victimized by predators disguised as entertainment executives.

A lot of attention has been focused on R. Kelly given his current legal circumstances. It is sad that the state of Florida was blind enough to eject charges brought against R. Kelly. Or, was it a mistake? Again, a case where a child was involved in sex with R. Kelly, and where physical proof existed, a child is blatantly victimized by an alleged predator, and the legal system.

Remember that R. Kelly is not the only male who has sought to engage in sex with children. There are other major rap stars who have done the same, and have sought to brag about it by making reference to the acts in their songs.

R. Kelly, in his pursuits, was rarely alone, and his methods were pervasive. So, does one really think that no one else knew of his activities with children? Did R. Kelly's assistants, producers, security, band mates, press and the record company know a bizarre recreation was taking place? Of course, many of those around R. Kelly knew what was going on because they too were part of the activities and an associated cover-up.

Jive Records certainly knew of R. Kelly's activities because I spoke with someone about my suspicions long before a scandal ensued. Not to mention, Jive Records was already familiar with the fact that R. Kelly became romantically involved with Aaliyah. R. Kelly had a history of sexual involvement with young girls even before Aaliyah, and this was never a secret among employees at Jive Records, as well as employees from Kelly's private entourage. In addition, Kelly had previously settled several legal claims that were brought against him. My question would be why these victims were not of the position to pursue criminal charges against the self-proclaimed "Pied Piper". The law should insist on mandatory criminal prosecution in such cases even when there is a financial payment to the family of a pedophile's victim.

Kelly's entourage was already familiar that Kelly has been known to make trips to local McDonald's restaurants, particularly those with playgrounds. Kelly met several kids at McDonald's restaurants and befriended them. There is no way of knowing exactly which of these children discussed with their parents that R. Kelly had become a "close" acquaintance. However, any parent should have been more inquisitive under the circumstances. It still amazes me how parents still would allow their children to be in the company of someone who developed a history of physical involvement with children.

In addition to R. Kelly's entourage being aware of his juvenile exploits, I happen to know that the record company was made aware of the seriousness of Kelly's fancies because a phone call was made to Clive Calder, and this phone call was placed by me. After navigating the endless barrage of assistants and assistants to assistants, we were able to have a conversation, and my report was made. Calder told me to leave my information with his assistance and that someone would contact me. Of course, I never received that phone call. Eventually, the urge to make contact once more ensued. But this time my calls were even less welcome than they had been before. Calder's assistant hung up on me, and Calder still never returned the call. It was obvious what was happening.

My calls to Jive Records continued, and eventually I reached R. Kelly's personal publicist, however, no one cared to listen to my concerns. And this is long before any of the big scandals occurred. Not even the Chicago Police Department was willing to entertain the idea. Everyone in the music business I could speak with was bombarded with my perspective, and people who had children whom they wanted to work with Kelly, had a change of heart. The parent of one rising star in the music business told me that she was planning to contact R. Kelly to have him produce a song. My immediate response was PLEASE DON'T DO THAT! Regarding any child I am adamant that Kelly should not have to work in close proximity to them. The record company, representatives, managers and publicists will say anything so that Kelly gets what he wants. After all, Barry Hankerson was the uncle of Aaliyah, and not even this stopped Kelly from molesting her innocence. How convenient it was for Aaliyah to be killed in a tragic plane crash just when authorities were asking more questions about Kelly's exploits with children.

About the Author

Terence McPhaul, author of the critically acclaimed treatise on celebrity behavior *The Celebrity Psyche,* is founder and director of McPhaul Consultants and Personal Advisors, an agency providing counseling, therapy, life coaching and personal advisor services exclusively for celebrities.

The creator of LeSerenite Wellness Center, and the Annual Managing Success and Celebrity conference, McPhaul initiated a curriculum that is used to provide new and veteran celebrities with the tools to navigate stardom from the perspective of one's emotional health.

Before returning to graduate school to earn a degree in Counseling Psychology, this Red Carpet regular was a Hazardous Materials Chemist. He has been utilized as a consultant for cinema, particularly by those seeking appropriate direction on projects with regard to psychological implications. McPhaul is regularly sought by program directors of TV talk shows and national media as an expert in the field of Mental Health to deliver perspective or respond to programming regarding social and behavioral issues.

McPhaul has appeared as a Mental Health expert for *Court TV,* and Bill O'Reilly's *The O'Reilly Factor for FOX News.*

Terence McPhaul resides in Atlanta, Georgia where he is a board member of several non-profit organizations.

978-0-595-35152-7
0-595-35152-2

Printed in the United Kingdom
by Lightning Source UK Ltd.
123077UK00002BA/275/A